Maximize Your IRA

Maximize Your IRA

NEIL DOWNING

Dearborn
Financial Publishing, Inc.®

This publication is designed to provide accurate and authoritative information in regard to the subject matter covered. It is sold with the understanding that the publisher is not engaged in rendering legal, accounting, or other professional service. If legal advice or other expert assistance is required, the services of a competent professional person should be sought.

Editorial Director: Cynthia A. Zigmund
Managing Editor: Jack Kiburz
Interior Design: Elizandro Carrington
Cover Design: Salvatore Concialdi
Typesetting: Elizabeth Pitts

Library of Congress Cataloging-in-Publication Data

Downing, Neil.
  Maximize your IRA/by Neil Downing
      p. cm.
    Includes index.
    ISBN 0-7931-2853-6 (pbk.)
      1. Individual retirement accounts—United States.   2. Retirement income—United States.   I. Title.
  HG1660.U5D68   1998
  332.024′01—dc21   98-13650
                                                  CIP

Dedication

For my wife, Vicki-Ann, and our children, James, Andrew, and Caitlin, whose love, patience, and good humor made this possible.

Contents

Preface   xi

Acknowledgments   xiii

1 The New Choice in IRAs   1

When IRAs Were King   1
Turning Back the Clock   2
A Picture of Confusion   3
Popularity Plunges   4
IRAs Return to the Spotlight   4
More Options Now   4
To Sum Up . . .   6
For More Information . . .   6

2 Putting Your Financial House in Order   7

The Big Picture   7
Your Personal Balance Sheet   8
Your Income Statement   10
Making the Most of Your
    Savings   13
Long-Range Goals   14
Where IRAs Fit In   15
Estimating Your Retirement
    Needs   16
Deductible IRAs and Roth
    IRAs   17
Nondeductible IRAs   18
To Sum Up . . .   18
For More Information . . .   18

3 Cashing In on IRA Tax Breaks   20

IRA Tax Breaks   21
The Government Pays You
    to Save   23
Another Tax Benefit   23
Postponing the Tax Bill   23
Why IRAs Make Sense   25
To Sum Up . . .   25
For More Information . . .   25

4 Do You Qualify for an IRA?   26

Got a Job? Get an IRA   26
Dollar Limit   26
Age Limit   27
Watch the Deadline   28
The Two-Part Test   29
Congress Changes the Rules   31
Figuring Your IRA Deduction:
    A Handy Formula   34
To Sum Up . . .   35
For More Information . . .   36

5 Where to Invest Your IRA Dollars   37

An Outline of Your Rights   37
Where to Open an Account   38
Your Investment Options   40
Professional Management and
    Diversification   41
How to Pick a Mutual Fund   42
Picking a Stock Brokerage   43
More Options   44
Even More Investment
    Choices   46
IRAs Don't Stand Alone   47
The Importance of Your
    Time Horizon   47
To Sum Up . . .   48
For More Information . . .   49

6 Managing Your IRA   50

Avoiding Fees   50
Most Fees Don't Qualify
    for a Deduction   51
Transferring Your IRA   52
Rolling Over Your IRA   52
The Flexibility of IRAs   55

The Choice Is Yours   55
Switching from Pensions to
    IRAs   56
When IRAs Are Not the Best
    Choice   57
A Conduit IRA   58
To Sum Up . . .   59
For More Information . . .   59

**7 Withdrawing Money from
    Your IRA   60**

Three Main Exits   60
Under 59½: Avoiding
    the Penalty   61
Between 59½ and 70½:
    The Tax Consequences   66
Over 70½: When You Must
    Withdraw   68
To Sum Up . . .   70
For More Information . . .   70

**8 Figuring Your Minimum
    Withdrawals   71**

A Summary of the Rules   71
The First Withdrawal   72
How Much You Must
    Withdraw   74
Choosing a Method   79
A Few Pointers   80
Helpful Hints   83
To Sum Up . . .   84
For More Information . . .   85

9 Planning Your Estate   86

Naming a Beneficiary   86
Complications When Choosing
    a Beneficiary   87
Federal Estate Tax   88
Some Estate Tax Relief   88
Elimination of Basis with
    IRAs   89
What Triggers Income Tax   90
The Beneficiary's Relationship with
    the IRA Owner   91
The Importance of Planning
    Ahead   93
Helpful Hints   94

To Sum Up . . .   95
For More Information . . .   95

10 Nondeductible IRAs   96

Taxes Are Key   96
How a Nondeductible IRA
    Can Help   97
Advantages of Nondeductible
    IRAs   98
How the Rules Work   99
When a Nondeductible IRA
    Can Help   101
Considering Your Options   102
To Sum Up . . .   103
For More Information . . .   103

11 The Education IRA   104

Is It a Good Idea?   104
A Few Problems   105
Understanding the Tax
    Breaks   107
Income Limits   107
Limits on the Type of
    School   108
Cashing In on the Benefits   108
Obey the Limits   109
When It's Time to
    Withdraw   109
The Closing Bell   110
Will It Work for You?   110
More Points to Consider   111
Consider the Alternatives   112
Other Choices   113
To Sum Up . . .   114
For More Information . . .   116

12 The Roth IRA   117

A Quick Look at Benefits   117
A Look at the Details   118
The Fine Print   120
A Few More Rules   121
How to Qualify for
    TaxBenefits   121
When Earnings Get Taxed   124
Recapping the Withdrawal
    Rules   125
Is the Roth IRA for You?   126

Roth IRAs versus Traditional
   IRAs   128
A Few Guidelines   129
Some Final Points   135
To Sum Up . . .   136
For More Information . . .   137

**13 Converting to a
   Roth IRA   139**

Tempting Tax Breaks   139
A Tax Is Still a Tax   140
How to Convert   141
Limits on Roth
   Conversions   142
Options When Switching from
   Your Classic IRA   145
When the Clock Starts
   to Tick   146
Avoiding Tax and Penalty   146
Should You Convert?   147
Putting It All Together   151
To Sum Up . . .   153
For More Information . . .   153

**14 Which IRA Is Right
   for You?   154**

The Traditional IRA   154
The Education IRA   155
The Roth IRA   156
The Nondeductible IRA   156
Are IRAs Always a
   Good Idea?   157
Disadvantages of IRAs   157
Benefits of IRAs   161
To Sum Up . . .   166

**Appendix A:
How IRAs Have Evolved   167**

**Appendix B:
Life Expectancy Tables   168**

Index   181

Preface

The bombshell struck just outside of Boston in a condominium owned by my friend the accountant.

It was April 1986. My wife and I had been married less than a year. And during that brief time our thoughts were mainly about ourselves—the gifts we had received, the honeymoon we had taken, and our plans for the future. The last thing on our minds was taxes.

We weren't prepared for what our accountant told us that night. With two incomes but no house, no mortgage, no children, and little else to deduct, we would face a huge tax bill. We didn't want to pay it but there seemed no option. What could we do?

Our accountant solved the dilemma by offering these three words: individual retirement account.

We had heard something about individual retirement accounts—IRAs. The newspapers and magazines were filled with advertisements and promotions. Still, we weren't sure how they worked. By the time the accountant explained what IRAs were all about and how they could save us money, we were sold.

The next night, with the tax filing deadline just a few hours away, we drove to the city's financial district. An investor center run by Fidelity Investments, the mutual fund giant, had stayed open late for last-minute business.

There, surrounded by other procrastinators, we opened an IRA for each of us. We mailed our tax returns a little while later and then drove home relieved and our tax problem was solved.

Millions of other Americans had done the same thing. By pouring money into IRAs, taxpayers not only saved for their retirement years, but also cut their tax bills. It was a sweet deal. And it was too good to last.

Later that year, Congress passed the Tax Reform Act of 1986 and slammed the door on what had become one of the most popular investments in the country.

IRAs would still exist, but Congress had changed the rules. As a result, IRAs lost their luster. Contributions plunged, mainly because they could no longer be deducted by many middle-class Americans.

With far fewer dollars flowing into IRAs, advertising dried up. Once a popular tool in almost everybody's financial plan, the IRA now seemed to withdraw to a quiet corner of the investment world.

Ten years later the picture began to change. In the summer of 1996, Congress opened the door a crack by offering more ways to tap your IRA without penalty. And a few more taxpayers became eligible to make full annual contributions.

The next summer Congress threw the door wide open. IRA contributions became fully deductible once again for millions of middle-class Americans. The government created new kinds of IRAs and made new rules for traditional IRAs. Congress allowed you to continue using IRAs to save for retirement, but you could also use them to save for college or to buy a new home. The changes became law when President Clinton signed the Taxpayer Relief Act of 1997.

But as the appeal of IRAs has grown, so too have the complications with the many more choices now available. The rules are trickier, and unless you can figure them out, you could lose a big opportunity.

Purpose of This Book

This book is a kind of owner's manual for IRAs. It's a plain-language guide written not for financial professionals but for the average consumer. It's intended to help you understand what IRAs are, how they work, and how they can best work for you. You'll find out which IRAs fit best in your financial plan, how to avoid tax and investment traps, and how best to manage your IRA—in your working years on through retirement.

The first chapter is an overview that touches on some of the new features of the traditional IRA and highlights some of the new IRAs now available. Chapter 2 offers tips on getting your financial house in order before you start to consider the various types of IRAs.

Chapters 3 through 10 focus entirely on the traditional IRA. Here you'll find out how the "classic" IRA works, where to invest your IRA dollars, how to cut fees, when to withdraw money, how to sort through tax complications, how to pick a beneficiary, how to deal with an IRA you inherit, and whether there's still a place in your portfolio for the nondeductible IRA.

Education IRAs and Roth IRAs

The second section of the book takes a close look at the new IRAs, how they work, and how they might benefit you. Chapter 11 looks at the new education IRA, Chapter 12 explains the Roth IRA, and Chapter 13 examines the potential benefits and pitfalls of converting a traditional IRA to a Roth IRA.

The final chapter brings it all together by looking at exactly which IRA might fit best in your financial picture and offers some alternatives to IRAs.

In Appendix B you'll find the official tables you'll need to figure minimum withdrawals from traditional IRAs.

You don't have to read the entire book in one sitting. Choose a chapter that interests you and then put the book aside to pick up later. It's intended as a handy reference to help you save money for your long-term goals, cut your tax bill, and maximize your IRA. Enjoy!

Acknowledgments

My thanks to the staff of Universal Pensions and *The IRA Reporter* newsletter; Mark Luscombe, Nicholas Kaster, Mary Dale Walters, and the staff at CCH Inc.; Bob Rywick and the staff at RIA Group; Andrew Wexler and the staff at Lande Communications; Dallas Salisbury and the staff at the Employee Benefit Research Institute; Pattie Schiele; Barbara C. Shuckra; Dana Gagne, CFP; Patricia A. Thompson, CPA, CFP; Jordan E. Goodman, founder and president of Amherst Enterprises and "The Money Answers" consumer information group; Brian S. Mattes and the staff at the Vanguard Group; Steven E. Norwitz and the staff at T. Rowe Price; Robert J. Glovsky and the faculty, staff, and students of the Boston University Program for Financial Planners; Stephen Hamblett, Joel P. Rawson, Carol J. Young, Thomas E. Heslin, Peter Phipps, John Kostrzewa, and the rest of the staff at the *Providence Journal-Bulletin,* as well as former editors James V. Wyman and James K. Sunshine, for making the "MoneyLine" column possible and thanks to the column's many readers, whose questions and comments inspired this book; and most of all my thanks to Cynthia Zigmund and the staff at Dearborn Financial Publishing.

The New Choice in IRAs

In the early 1980s, IRAs were king of the investment world until Congress closed the door and their popularity plunged. Now IRAs have been born again. The traditional IRA has a new style with lots of new tax benefits, and new types of IRAs are adding excitement.

Behold the new IRA!

It once dwelled in the shadow of its popular and much-publicized cousins, such as the 401(k) plan and other retirement programs. Now the individual retirement account has become, once again, a snazzy new way to save. It's more widely available—and much more appealing—to millions of Americans.

It wasn't always that way. Created in 1974 as part of landmark legislation to expand and safeguard employee retirement plans, IRAs were originally intended only to help those who weren't covered by pension plans at work. As a result, IRAs initially were used only by a sliver of the population.

Through a tax law change in 1981, however, Congress made IRAs available to just about anybody—regardless of whether you had a pension plan at work and no matter how much money you earned.

When IRAs Were King

For one brief shining period in the 1980s as a result of the change in the tax law, IRAs reigned supreme. If you opened a newspaper, read a magazine, listened to the radio, or watched TV during that time, the message was hard to miss: IRAs were a great way to save, and you just had to take advantage.

IRAs offered a heady mixture of tax and investment benefits that were hard to find anyplace else. And Americans found them irresistible. Banks, credit unions, and others trumpeted the IRA, and it was an easy point to make: open an IRA and get an income tax deduction.

Imagine! Just dump some money in an IRA—even if you were merely transferring it from a regular savings account—and you could claim a deduction on your federal income tax return, cutting your tax bill.

In effect, the government used IRAs to encourage Americans to save money for their retirement. And the government was even willing to help foot part of the bill by offering a tax subsidy. What's more, your money could grow each year without being taxed; the only time you'd have to pay a tax was when you made a withdrawal.

Big Tax Benefits

Because IRAs were set up as long-range savings plans, you would probably make withdrawals only after you retired, when your income was lower and your tax rate lower too.

You didn't have to be an accountant to see how IRAs could work for you. The benefits were staring you in the face every day. All you had to do was open an account, plunk down your money, and you were in business.

Were IRAs popular? The numbers tell the story. In 1981, when IRA use was restricted (and before the new law took effect), only about 3.4 million tax returns claimed deductions for IRAs. But in 1982, the first time IRAs became widely available, the number of returns claiming an IRA deduction nearly quadrupled, to 12 million. And government records show that the amount of IRA deductions, which totaled just $4.8 billion in 1981, leaped to $28.3 billion the following year.

As the message was repeated, more taxpayers made their move. But with the Taxpayer Relief Act of 1986, Congress took away the punch bowl, as shown dramatically in Figure 1.1.

Turning Back the Clock

In effect, the government turned back the clock by making IRAs available mainly for those who weren't covered by a pension plan at work. That's how IRAs had begun, and that's what the new rules said. If you weren't covered by a regular retirement plan at work, then you could contribute to an IRA and still claim a federal income tax deduction.

But what if you *were* covered by a retirement plan at work? That's where the government got strict. Sure, you could still contribute to an IRA; but if you were already taking part in an employer-sponsored pension plan, you could claim an income tax deduction only if your income fell below certain limits.

Figure 1.1   When IRAs Were King

Created in 1974, individual retirement accounts weren't widely available until 1982. After 1986, however, Congress restricted their use and their popularity waned.

Year	Number of Tax Returns Claiming IRA Deductions (in millions)	Total IRA Deductions (in billions)
1980	2.6	3.4
1981	3.4	4.8
1982	12.0	28.3
1983	13.6	32.1
1984	15.2	35.4
1985	16.2	38.2
1986	15.5	37.8
1987	7.3	14.1
1988	6.4	11.9
1989	5.8	10.8
1990	5.2	9.9
1991	4.7	9.0
1992	4.5	8.7
1993	4.4	8.5
1994	4.3	8.4

Source: U.S. House Ways and Means Committee

Suddenly the test for IRA tax deduction eligibility depended on your income. Well, not on your income, really, but on your adjusted gross income. No, wait: not your adjusted gross income—your *modified* adjusted gross income.

A Picture of Confusion

The new rule left lots of taxpayers scratching their heads. Unless you were an accountant or used an accountant, it was hard to figure whether you could claim a deduction for making an IRA contribution.

True, most Americans were still eligible to claim the IRA tax deduction despite the new income restrictions. But that point didn't hit home because the message was no longer clear—it had become clouded by a bunch of new rules, tables, and worksheets.

Taxpayers grew discouraged and, as a result, a lot of people who could have gotten full benefit for plopping money into an IRA just didn't bother. IRAs had become too complicated.

Popularity Plunges

There was still more bad news. Buried in the 1986 tax law was a ticking time bomb: the income limits to qualify for an IRA tax deduction weren't indexed to increase with inflation each year. They were fixed. So even if you were among the lucky ones who clearly understood how the new rules worked and you hoped to keep making a deductible contribution to your IRA each year, odds were that at some point your plans would be shattered.

Why was this so? Because while your overall income rose each year—through pay raises, promotions, or a better job—the income limits stayed the same. As each year passed, therefore, more taxpayers were denied a tax deduction. Thus, the appeal of IRAs diminished as time went on.

IRAs Return to the Spotlight

With the Taxpayer Relief Act of 1997, IRAs were born again. The government changed the rules, making IRAs a lot more attractive. They still aren't as attractive as they once were, though. If you're covered by a pension plan at work, for example, you still must pass the two-part test. And the overall amount you may contribute to an IRA each year remains $2,000 per person, the same as it was in 1981, so its value has been eroded by time and inflation.

More Options Now

The new law nevertheless gave taxpayers a whole new range of options: new rules for traditional IRAs, new ways to withdraw money from your IRA without paying a penalty, and new kinds of IRAs.

Here's a peek at what the IRA landscape looks like today:

- The income limits for the traditional IRA are on the rise. This means that more taxpayers each year will be able to claim a federal income tax deduction for the amount they contribute to a traditional IRA—even if they're covered by a pension plan at work. For some taxpayers, then, it'll be just like the old days again. For instance, if you were single in 1997, you generally were able to claim the full IRA deduction only if your adjusted gross income was below $25,000. The new law increased this limit to $30,000 for 1998, $31,000 for 1999, and $32,000 for 2000; and it'll keep increasing every year until it reaches $50,000 in 2005. What if you're married and file a joint income tax return? For 1997 you generally were able to claim the full deduction only if your adjusted gross income was below $40,000. The new law boosted that limit to $50,000 for 1998, $51,000 for 1999, and $52,000 for 2000; and it'll keep jumping every year until it levels off at $80,000 in 2007. (See Chapter 4.)

- Many more homemakers will be able to make fully deductible contributions to IRAs. Under the old rules, a so-called nonworking spouse couldn't claim a deduction for an IRA contribution if the working spouse took part in a pension plan at work. Under the new rules, a working spouse's pension plan won't matter; the nonworking spouse will generally be able to claim a full deduction as long as the couple's adjusted gross income is less than $150,000. (For details, see Chapter 4.)

- There are now more ways to withdraw money from a traditional IRA without being penalized. Under the old rules, you'd generally have to pay a 10 percent penalty if you withdrew money before you reached age 59½. The penalty was waived if the withdrawal was made because of death or disability, or if the money was part of a series of regular, equal withdrawals made over your lifetime. Congress has steadily added to the list of exceptions. For instance, you're now able to withdraw money penalty-free if you use the money to pay for health insurance or medical expenses (under certain conditions). And you may now withdraw money penalty-free if you use the proceeds to pay for college tuition and expenses or to buy your first home. Even though you must meet the rules to escape the penalty, withdrawing money from an IRA today isn't quite so painful as it used to be. (For details, see Chapter 7.)

- A new kind of IRA, called the Roth IRA, lets you withdraw money tax-free. You can't get an income tax deduction for contributing to a Roth IRA, but if you meet the rules, you may withdraw money from a Roth IRA—including all the money your account has earned over the years—free of income tax *and* penalty. The highest you may contribute to a Roth IRA each year is $2,000 if you're single or $4,000 if you're married and filing jointly. (See Chapter 12 for details.)

- Even if you don't—or can't—contribute to a Roth IRA, you may still be able to transfer money to one from a traditional IRA. You'll have to pay income tax on the money that you transfer, or roll over, to the Roth IRA, but you won't have to pay a penalty, even if you transfer the money before you reach 59½. And if you meet the rules, the money can be withdrawn later without triggering tax *or* penalties. For money transferred to a Roth IRA from a traditional IRA in 1998, a special tax rule applies: You won't have to include the entire amount of the transfer on your tax return for 1998; instead, you may spread it out over four years, softening the tax impact you'd otherwise face if you had to report it as income in a lump sum in a single tax year. (See Chapter 13 for details.)

- Another new kind of IRA, the education IRA, lets you set aside up to $500 a year as a kind of trust fund to help pay for a child's college expenses. You can't take a tax deduction for the money you contribute, but the money may later be withdrawn—tax-free and penalty-free—if it's used to pay for the beneficiary's college tuition, fees, room and board, and certain other expenses. Although you can't contribute more than $500 a year to an education IRA, you generally may have as many education IRAs as you have children and contribute up to $500 to each account. If the student doesn't use up all the money in his or her account by graduation, later withdrawals will generally be taxed and slapped with a 10 percent penalty, but this can be avoided if the student transfers the account balance to another beneficiary in the same family. (For details, see Chapter 11.)

To Sum Up . . .

As you can see, the world of IRAs has changed dramatically in a fairly short time. Created in 1974 only for a limited number of taxpayers who had no pension plans, IRAs commanded center stage in the early 1980s, when nearly everyone was eligible to open an account and claim a deduction. A 1986 law, however, sharply restricted their use. But now IRAs are back in the spotlight with new rules to make them more appealing, and some new types have been introduced too.

Each change, however, comes with a whole new set of complications. To help you sort through the details and decide if any of these IRAs have a place in your family's financial picture, this book takes a close look at each option, explaining them in plain language with examples, tables, and tips.

For More Information . . .

The Vanguard Group of mutual funds, of Valley Forge, Pennsylvania, has a free booklet on the tax law that made so many changes to IRAs. *Understanding the Taxpayer Relief Act of 1997* is a plain-language guide that not only looks at the law's impact on IRAs but also reviews tax credits for families with children, the new capital gains tax rates, saving for a child's education, and planning your estate.

For your free copy, call Vanguard at 1-800-523-8552, or write: Vanguard, P.O. Box 2600, Valley Forge, PA 19482. If you have access to a computer, you may read this and other information at the company's World Wide Web site at www.vanguard.com.

Putting Your Financial House in Order

Before you pick an IRA, before you even settle on a long-range goal, you need to organize your finances in two easy steps by creating a personal balance sheet and cash flow statement. This chapter shows you how to put these statements together and then analyze them to cut your expenses, save more money, and use them to set long-range goals so you can see how IRAs can fit into your own financial plan.

It's almost overwhelming—new rules for old IRAs and the availability of new types of IRAs. Which should you pick? Should you have more than one? Or none at all?

These are key questions, but with only a little effort you can answer them yourself. All you have to do is a bit of paperwork, then a little soul-searching.

The Big Picture

There's no point worrying about which IRA is best for you if you don't have your overall financial condition in order first. Why spend time picking out new wallpaper if your roof has just sprung a dozen leaks? Best to take care of the structure first before worrying about the ornaments.

Maybe you're the sort of person who keeps track of every penny you take in and every cent you spend. It's all there on a neat little computer program, with copies on disks that are securely stowed in a safe-deposit box. If so, that's great. You're way ahead of the game. But if you're like most people, odds are you could stand to do a little financial housecleaning.

Before you consider picking an IRA, before you even start to think about long-term savings plans at all, you need to look first at the big picture. The point is you should not look at an IRA investment in isolation on its own.

Look instead at your overall financial picture to see where—or even *if*—an IRA would fit in and what sorts of investments you should make with your IRA dollars. An IRA will help you only if it's part of an overall financial plan.

If you haven't already done so, take the time now to put together a personal balance sheet for your household. This is simply a snapshot of your true financial condition at a single point in time—a list of all your assets and all your debts. While you're at it, make a cash flow statement too, for it shows where your household's money comes from and where it's spent.

If you're single, the job is easy: it's just your assets, debts, income, and expenses. If there's more than one person in your household—if you're married, for example—the job is a little more difficult because you've got to collect information for two people or more if you have children or other relatives living with you.

No matter how much information you have to collect to get the job done right, it's easier if you use some basic records. Get out your income tax returns, life insurance policies, pension or profit-sharing statements, mutual fund account records, checking account statements, charge account statements, and other such records to use as a reference. They will help ensure that you use the right numbers, and they'll also help the job go more quickly.

Your Personal Balance Sheet

To make a balance sheet, just get a pencil and a sheet of paper; it's not that hard. Figure 2.1 shows a sample balance sheet. Feel free to use it as a guide or as a starting point. Follow these two steps:

1. On one side, list all your *assets*, starting with the value of all your big-ticket items, such as your house and car. Include any investments you may have, such as stocks, bonds, and mutual funds, and retirement plans at work. Also be sure to list your cash assets—that is, assets that could be quickly converted to cash, such as your savings and checking accounts, money market accounts, and the cash value of life insurance policies. Don't forget to list all your other assets, such as furnishings, appliances, art, antiques, jewelry, and the like. Try to use only current market values, and jot down the value next to each asset on your list. (If you can't get exact figures—on a piece of furniture or on that old TV set, for example—just use your best guess.)
2. On the other side of the ledger, show all your *debts*, including any mortgage loans, car loans, and charge card accounts. Show the current balance for each.

Figure 2.1   Your Household Balance Sheeet

**Your Household Balance Sheet
As of Dec. 31 (insert year)**

Assets   **Debts**

Cash and Cash Equivalents:

Checking account   Balance on mortgage
Bank savings account   Balance on car loan
Money market fund   Balance on credit cards
Life insurance cash value

Total: **Total:**

Invested Assets:

IRAs
Pension plans
Mutual funds
Stocks

Total:

Personal Use Assets:

House(s)
Car(s)
Personal property

Total:

Total Assets: **Total Debts:**

**Your Household's Net Worth:
(Total Assets minus Total Debts)**

Note: List the fair market value of each asset as of the date of your balance sheet. List only the vested portion of your pension plans (the amount you've earned the right to receive). For "Personal property" use the fair market value of all other assets you own, including furniture, jewelry, appliances, television sets and other electronics, camper and other recreational vehicles, and other items. (It may help to create a separate list of personal property assets to use as a supplement.) List only the principal part of your mortgage loan, car loan, credit card, and other debts.

Once you've finished with these numbers, you can easily figure out your personal net worth: simply subtract your total debts from your total assets. This number shows your true bottom line. In effect, it tells you how much would be left over if you had to sell all your assets and pay off all your debts at once. Companies do this all the time. It's really helpful if you can do it once a year to see how your personal wealth has grown (or fallen!) over time.

It's called a "balance sheet" because the figures on your sheet must, in the end, balance out. Compiling a balance sheet isn't as complicated as it sounds; it's really just an accounting maneuver. On one side of the sheet is the value of your assets. On the other side is the current amount of all your debts. The difference is your net worth. To balance your sheet, just add your net worth to your debts; the resulting sum is equal to the total value of all your assets. Your financial statement is now balanced. Easy!

Your Income Statement

Next, put together your own personal income statement, or statement of cash flow, for the most recent year. This is kind of like a checking account except that it's much bigger. It includes all the money that flows *into* your household from all places over the span of an entire year. It also includes all the money that flows *out of* your household over the same period.

To put together a personal income statement, take another sheet of paper. Figure 2.2 shows a sample cash flow statement that you may want to use as a guide or as a starting point. Here are two steps to follow:

1. On one side, list the sources and amounts of your annual income, or *inflows,* including wages, salaries, tips, commissions, and bonuses; dividends you get from stocks, bonds, and mutual funds; interest you earn from savings and checking accounts; and any other money that you (or any other members of your household) take in each year, including earnings from side jobs and part-time work. (Be sure to include any withdrawals you made from savings or other such sources; these count too.)

2. On the other side, show your annual spending, or *outflows,* listing each place where your money goes. Include expenditures for big-ticket items, mortgage or rent payments, car loan payments, and all your insurance premiums. Use separate entries, too, for such other items as taxes (including federal and state income tax). Don't forget to list excise taxes, property tax, and Social Security tax. Make separate entries for the money you spend on food, utilities, clothing, vacations, entertainment, and miscellaneous items. Remember also to list how much, if any, you managed to save and invest, and how much went

Figure 2.2   Your Household Cash Flow Statement

**Your Household Cash Flow Statement
For Year Ended Dec. 31 (insert year)**

Money Flowing In
    Salaries (before tax)
    Interest from savings accounts, CDs
    Interest from money market accounts
    Dividends (from stocks, mutual funds)
    Withdrawals from savings
Total:

Money Flowing Out
    Savings and investments
        Total savings and investments:
    Fixed outflows
        Mortgage payments
        Car loan payments
        Real estate tax
        Insurance premiums
        Total fixed outflows:
    Variable outflows
        Federal, state, local income tax
        Social Security tax
        Food, drink (including dining out)
        Utilities, other household expenses
        Transportation (include gas, maintenance for car)
        Entertainment, vacations
        Out-of-pocket medical, dental expenses
        Clothing, shoes, haircuts, personal care
        Charitable contributions
        Hobby expenses
        Miscellaneous
        Total variable outflows:
Total:

Note: Cash outflows and inflows must balance exactly. For "Salaries" include gross amount of wages, salaries, commissions, bonuses, etc. For "Savings and investments" remember to include deposits to bank accounts and money market funds, plus your own contributions to pensions, profit-sharing plans, and IRAs. "Mortgage payments" should include principal and interest only. "Insurance premiums" are for car, homeowner, life, medical, disability, and other insurance policies. "Miscellaneous" includes all other items, such as withdrawals from automated teller machines (ATMs) and other spending.

into each account. If you can't break out all the items you charged during the year, lump them together under "Miscellaneous." And don't be put off because you have to figure your income and expenses for the entire year. To make the job easier, break it into smaller chunks— weekly or monthly, for instance—and use your checking account register, credit card statements, pay stubs, and similar records.

Studying the Numbers

Once you've finished these steps, sit back and smile because most of the hard work is over. Now all you need to do is look closely at the numbers on each sheet and listen carefully to what they're telling you. You don't have to be an accountant to do this; just use your common sense.

Take a look first at your income statement. If you're spending more than you're taking in, you're in trouble. Scrutinize each line item to try to spot some expenses you may be able to trim.

If you're dining out a lot, for example, even just at fast-food joints, perhaps you could resolve to eat more meals at home to save money. Buying lunch? Why not bring a sandwich to work. Spending a lot on faraway vacation spots? Maybe you can trim this budget item by traveling closer to home in the future. Charge accounts too high? If you pay off your balance in full each month, you'll save money in finance charges. If you can't swing that right now, at least shop around for a card that'll charge you a lower interest rate. And if you have too many cards, get out the scissors, cut some (or all!) of your cards into tiny pieces and toss them away. This will help you avoid the temptation to spend.

Buy or lease?   Leasing a new car every two years? Think about buying one instead, and keep driving it until long after your payments have stopped. Mortgage payment too high? Shop around at various lenders to see if you could refinance at a lower rate, cutting your monthly payment. (You might also think about cutting the term of your loan, allowing you to save thousands of dollars in interest over the life of the loan.) Need a new outfit to replace worn or ill-fitting clothes? Skip the mall and browse at consignment or thrift shops.

You get the idea. The point is to use the sheet that you've put together to help you study carefully your saving and spending habits. Having all the numbers in front of you helps you see the picture more clearly and may give you the necessary ammunition to make some big decisions, especially those you may have been putting off.

Now look again at your balance sheet for help in focusing on the big picture. If you have more debts than assets, you're in big trouble and should consider taking some drastic steps. You may need to move to a smaller house to slash your mortgage debt or sell one of your cars to eliminate a car loan. And if such drastic steps don't help much, you may have to seek court protection from creditors under federal bankruptcy law while you try to sort out your financial affairs. (Talk with a lawyer or debt counselor first to review your options.)

Making the Most of Your Savings

Even if you've got more assets than debts, you may still be able to make some improvements. For instance, are you making the most of the money you save? If you've got a pile of money sitting in a low-rate passbook savings account, switch to other investment options, such as money market mutual funds, to generate more interest income.

If you've got a big balance in a checking account, try shopping around among banks, thrifts, and credit unions for a better deal. You may find one that'll require a lower minimum balance before fees are applied, thus freeing up some money that you can save elsewhere and giving you a higher return.

Your balance sheet will also help you make key long-term decisions about your household's financial situation. For example:

- What if you've got a lot of money salted away in retirement plans at work or in stocks, bonds, and mutual funds, but you've got little cash available? This could spell trouble if you were to lose your job or suffer a long-term illness or disability, so you may want to take the time now to rearrange your investments and make sure you've got enough money readily available to handle emergencies (experts sometimes recommend enough money to cover three to six months of expenses and keeping this money in short-term, conservative investments, such as bank accounts, money market funds, U.S. Treasury bills, or U.S. savings bonds).

- Take a broad look at your overall investment portfolio to see if it's out of balance. If most or all of your money is invested in stocks or stock mutual funds, you may be shouldering too much risk (depending on your age and other factors). If so, think about putting some of your money into bonds or bond mutual funds and some into short-term cash-oriented instruments. Remember: The stock market roared through the early to mid-1990s, breaking record after record. But markets tumble sometimes too. Your best strategy is to have a balance of investments so that you can profit when the market rises in value but won't suffer as much when the market declines.

- Do you have enough life insurance for your family? It's great to have a strong balance sheet with a lot of assets and little debt. But what will protect your loved ones when you die? Where will they turn to replace the income stream you would have provided in future years? Because you may not have enough assets to generate income sufficient to meet your household's long-term needs, think about adding to any life insurance coverage you already have. Even if you think you've got enough coverage, you may be carrying too much risk if most or all of your policies are provided through your job. What would happen to your coverage if you lost your job? Could you afford to continue the coverage by paying the premiums on your own? If you tried to get your own policy if you lost your job or changed jobs, would you be insurable? You may want to think about getting a policy on your own now, while you're healthy, and maybe even locking in a fixed premium by getting level-premium term insurance. Having enough money in cash types of investments is also important for estate planning issues: If you were to die soon, would there be enough cash available for the executor of your estate to pay tax, legal, and other expenses? Or would the person handling your estate's affairs have to start cashing in less liquid investments to foot the bill?

- Even if you've got enough life insurance coverage, do you have a disability policy? You stand a greater chance of suffering a long-term disability than of dying before you reach retirement, so it's worth looking into getting a long-term disability policy. Even if you have coverage at work, it may not be enough, and you may not be able to continue coverage for a long time if you were to lose your job.

Long-Range Goals

By now you've probably got your financial house in order, or you're a long way toward getting the job done. Now it's time to set some realistic goals and put together a written plan to make sure you meet your goals. This step can be tricky because there are a lot of variables and a lot of tax, legal, and other complications. You may want to enlist professional help from an accountant, a financial planner, or another adviser.

Everyone has goals. Maybe you're saving to buy a house, a vacation home, or a boat. Maybe you'd like to save to put your children through college. Perhaps you simply want to put together a nest egg you can use to help cover expenses during your retirement years. Or maybe you have a lot of different goals you'd like to reach.

Paying for Your Goals

As a first step, estimate how much each of your goals will cost. Do you have enough money already set aside to cover it? If not, how much would you need to save and invest to meet the goal? Could you squeeze enough out of your existing budget, or do you have to make some cuts? Can you meet all the goals you've set or just a few? Ultimately, you'll probably have to set priorities.

In other words, you may have to write down all your goals, then list which ones are the most important to you and which can be realistically achieved given how much you've saved or invested, how much you could pull out of your budget, and how many years you have left to try to reach your goal.

If you're nearing retirement and you've got little if any money set aside, for instance, then building a retirement nest egg may be your top priority. You've also got to search your soul to try to figure out how comfortable you'd be risking some of your money in various types of investments.

As you know, stocks (and stock mutual funds) generally offer the highest returns over the long haul, but they typically come with the most risk. The value of your investment could fall sharply at some point, so these types of investments are best only for long-term goals. Should a severe market downturn occur, your investment may need five to seven years or more to recover from the drop.

If, on the other hand, you can't stand the risk and you're comfortable only with the safest investments, such as bank accounts, you may not be able to reach your goals; you may have to scale back your objectives or find another way to pay for them, such as a second job.

Where IRAs Fit In

IRAs can help you reach your long-term goals, whether the goals involve buying a house, paying for a child's college education, or just ensuring a better lifestyle in retirement. But should you choose an IRA? If so, which type? And for what goal? These questions are answered in greater detail in the chapters ahead.

For now, it's important simply to study your personal financial picture carefully, set goals, then try to find the money to help you meet them. Even though IRAs can be used for lots of purposes, their main purpose is for retirement savings. Before you think about IRAs, however, look first at your goals for retirement and whether you can reach them.

The truth is that we're all living longer today. At one time only a small percentage of the population could expect to live beyond age 65. Today most Americans can expect to live far beyond that. This good news also means that the nation's Social Security program will be sorely taxed in the years ahead. Odds are that Social Security will still be there for you when you retire, even though it probably won't be available in the form it is today. People in the workforce today will probably have to work more years before they can qualify for full Social Security benefits, for example. And those benefits may not be enough to give you a comfortable lifestyle in retirement because the cost to the program will be too great with too many people drawing benefits and too few people contributing to the fund. As a result, you'll have to arrange to have some money set aside on your own.

How much should you set aside? To answer that question, you've got to figure out some other, more basic questions. For instance, when do you plan to retire, and how many years away from retirement are you? If you want to retire early, do you have enough money to reach the target? And no matter when you plan to retire, how will you cover your expenses?

Your first goal should be to estimate how much you'll spend in retirement. Odds are your annual expenses won't be as great as your spending needs before retirement. But there will be bills, and you'll have to find a way to pay them.

Does your employer provide health care coverage to retirees? Many don't, so you'll have to plan on paying for some sort of supplemental health care coverage and find a plan that meets your needs and your budget.

Where do you plan to live? Will you give up your house and buy or rent a smaller living space? Will you move to another state? If so, what are the tax consequences?

If you'll require care in a nursing home, or home health care, who'll pay? It may be time now to check the costs and other details of a long-term care insurance policy.

Estimating Your Retirement Needs

As you can see, it's important to at least estimate your retirement spending needs now. You'll also have to take inflation into account. Calculating all this stuff can be a big job. Fortunately, many mutual fund companies, insurance companies, and other organizations will supply you with free worksheets to help you calculate how much you'll spend in retirement and how much you'll need to save to get there. If you have access to a computer, you can do the calculations online or buy software programs that'll help you find the answers. Only after you get this basic groundwork done can you choose how you're going to save.

Once you've got the groundwork figured out, you can then think about the best types of accounts to use to meet your goals. IRAs can be a great help. But do you have a savings plan at work, one that lets you save money before taxes are taken out? If so, try to save the maximum amount. (This is especially true if your employer is willing to kick in some extra money on your behalf, in which case try to take full advantage.) In 1998, you can stash up to $10,000—before taxes—in a 401(k) or 403(b) retirement savings plan at work. (The limit is indexed to inflation, so it could rise in future years.)

If you've got a traditional type of pension at work (known as a "defined benefit" plan—one that guarantees you a fixed benefit when you retire), ask your plan sponsor for a current estimate of how much you can expect to receive at retirement.

Once you have an idea of how much you can save through programs offered by your employer, you can start to estimate how much money will be available when you retire. Then you can decide whether you'll have enough money to meet your goals.

Deductible IRAs and Roth IRAs

If you've fully funded your retirement savings plans at work, look next to IRAs. Which ones? If you qualify for the traditional deductible IRA—one that allows you to claim a federal income tax deduction for the amount you contribute—go for it. The combination of an immediate income tax deduction and the ability to save year after year on a tax-deferred basis is almost unbeatable.

Deductible IRAs are generally best if you can invest in a separate account the money that you save on taxes when you make your IRA contributions. They're also generally best if you expect to be in a lower income tax bracket when you retire—and most people *do* wind up in a lower bracket in retirement—unless Congress changes the rules! (When you withdraw money from a traditional IRA in retirement, you won't be penalized but the amount of each withdrawal is subject to income tax. That's why it's best if you're in a lower income tax bracket when you begin making your withdrawals.)

If you don't qualify for a fully deductible IRA, or if you qualify for only a partial income tax deduction, try to save in a Roth IRA. You won't get an immediate income tax deduction for the amount you contribute to a Roth account, but you won't be taxed as your money grows inside your account each year, and if you meet the rules, all your withdrawals will be tax-free and penalty-free. That's a mighty attractive feature, and it's why you've been hearing so much about Roth IRAs lately.

Nondeductible IRAs

If your income is so high you don't qualify for either a traditional deductible IRA or a Roth IRA, you can always salt away some money in a traditional nondeductible IRA. Here, too, you won't get an immediate income tax deduction, but as your money grows inside your account, the growth won't be taxed each year. And when you finally withdraw money in retirement, only the portion of each withdrawal that comes from earnings will generally be subject to tax.

To Sum Up . . .

IRAs can be a great way to save, but you can't consider them in isolation and make a decision as if nothing else mattered. There's no point worrying about which IRA is best for you if you don't first get a firm handle on how much you spend, how much you save, how much your assets are worth, and how much your total debts are. Once you've figured this out—once you look at the big picture by making your own personal balance sheet and cash flow statement—you can start to set long-term goals and figure out how to pay for them.

After these initial steps are taken, you can then choose which investment vehicles are best to help you reach your goals. Before you look at IRAs, make sure you fully fund the retirement savings plan you may have at work, especially if your employer is willing to contribute some money to it on your behalf. Then you can look at IRAs and decide whether to contribute to a traditional deductible IRA, a Roth IRA, or a traditional nondeductible IRA. (Coming chapters detail exactly how each of these IRAs and the education IRA work.)

For More Information . . .

- The Institute of Certified Financial Planners in Denver has several booklets and brochures that can help you analyze your household spending, put together a budget, and save for long-term goals. They include *Questions and Answers about . . . Financial Planning; How to Manage Your Financial Resources: Creating a Spending Plan You Can Control; Taking a Fiscal Inventory: How to Put Your Financial House in Order;* and *Selecting a Qualified Financial Planning Professional: 12 Questions to Consider.* For a free copy of the brochures and booklets, call 1-800-282-PLAN. You may also contact the group's Web site at this Internet address: www.icfp.org.

- *Everyone's Money Book,* 2nd edition (Dearborn Financial Publishing), by Jordan E. Goodman, is a clearly written, comprehensive book about issues relating to your money matters. It's a handy how-to guide on such topics as household budgeting; calculating, planning, and paying for retirement and other long-range goals; and money strategies for each stage of your life. It's available in bookstores or by calling 1-800-553-9997.
- T. Rowe Price Associates has published the *T. Rowe Price Retirement Planning Kit* for people who are more than five years away from retirement. It includes a workbook to help you figure how much money you'll need for retirement and how much you need to save to reach your goal. It also offers tips on putting together a retirement investment strategy. Another publication, the *T. Rowe Price Retirees Financial Guide,* is for those who have already retired or are close to retirement. It includes a workbook to help retirees estimate how much money they can afford to spend in retirement so they can maintain their standard of living. It takes into account taxes, inflation, and sources of retirement income, including Social Security. Both kits are available free by calling 1-800-541-8460 or by writing: T. Rowe Price, 100 East Pratt St., Baltimore, MD 21202.

Cashing In on IRA Tax Breaks

The traditional IRA is all about tax breaks because the government is willing to foot the bill to help you save. We get a close look in this chapter at what the tax breaks are, how they work, and how they can save you a lot of money.

The IRA is a way you can save for your retirement. You open an account, put in some money, let it be, and watch it grow. After you retire, you start to take the money out.

In some ways the IRA is just like any other savings account. So what's the big deal about IRAs? *Taxes.* IRAs offer some big tax benefits—and that's what makes these accounts so appealing.

If you qualify for the tax breaks, IRAs are almost magical, with benefits that make them practically irresistible. Doubtful?

Look at it this way: when you deposit money in a passbook savings account, for example, you get no tax break. Sure, your money earns interest. But every January the bank sends you a statement called a Form 1099 that shows how much interest your account earned over the past year. You have to report that interest on your federal income tax return, and you'll probably wind up paying taxes on it. The same thing happens the next year. And the next.

As long as your money is in a so-called taxable account, such as a regular bank savings account, all the interest you earn will be taxed. It'll be taxed by the federal government. And state and local governments may tax you, too, depending on where you live.

Think for a minute about what happens: odds are that the money you deposit in a bank account has already been taxed. Maybe it came out of your paycheck or from some other place where the tax man takes the first bite.

And when your account starts to earn interest, the interest itself gets taxed. In other words, you get whacked twice.

IRA Tax Breaks

Now look at the IRA. Instead of getting taxed twice, you may qualify for two tax breaks, which can save you money.

Putting money into an IRA is known as a "contribution," which is somewhat like a deposit; and when you contribute money to an IRA, chances are that you can use it to claim a tax deduction. (You can also transfer money to an IRA from a pension plan or another IRA, but that's a different matter and is the focus of a later chapter.)

Claiming Your Deduction

A deduction is, in effect, a reduction in the amount of income you report for tax purposes. It can lower your tax bill, even though it doesn't mean you actually earned less. It just means that you report to the IRS that you earned less than you really did.

The government taxes you, not on your actual earnings, but on your *reported* earnings after you subtract your deductions. And because the government taxes you on your reported earnings, not on your actual earnings, you save money in taxes.

By contributing money to an IRA, therefore, you can report to the government that you earned less than you really did. As a result, you pay less federal income tax than you ordinarily would, so an IRA contribution can help cut your tax bill.

If it sounds complicated, it really isn't. Here's an example: Suppose you're single and had $22,000 in income. To keep things simple, let's assume that all the money came from your job. (We'll ignore for now any of the usual deductions, exemptions, and other items that are part of a typical tax return.) In this example let's say you owe the federal government about $3,300 in income tax on your $22,000 in earnings. But suppose you put $2,000 into an IRA during the year. In that case, your entire $2,000 contribution is deductible.

Trimming your tax bill.   When it's time to report how much you earned for the year in our example, you can tell the IRS you made $20,000, not $22,000, and now you owe about $3,000 in income tax, a savings of $300. In other words, by making a $2,000 contribution to an IRA, you saved yourself $300 in income tax because the government wants to encourage people to save for their own retirement, and it's willing to give up some tax revenue to help citizens do the job.

A break for married couples.   Married couples can get the same sort of break. Suppose you're married, filing jointly, and your total income is $34,000.

To keep the example simple, let's again assume that all this money came from your jobs.

In this example, you might owe the federal government about $5,100 in income tax. But what if you and your spouse contribute $2,000 each to an IRA? In that case, the combined total of $4,000 in IRA contributions is fully deductible, so now you can report your earnings for the year to be $30,000, not $34,000.

As a result, you'll owe the federal government only about $4,500 in income tax. In other words, because each of you made a $2,000 fully deductible contribution to an IRA, you cut your federal income tax bill by $600.

Just One Move Saves You Money

Take a moment to think about what the above examples mean. By sticking $2,000 into a different kind of savings account—an IRA—the single taxpayer saves $300 in federal income tax in our example. And by salting away a total $4,000 in IRA contributions, the married couple filing jointly saves $600 in federal income tax in our example.

In other words, our imaginary taxpayers cut their tax bills simply by choosing to set aside some of their money in their own retirement accounts. How much you can cut your tax bill by contributing to an IRA depends on your tax bracket and is shown in Figure 3.1.

Figure 3.1   How an IRA Can Cut Your Tax Bill

If you contribute $2,000 to a traditional IRA, you may be able to claim a federal income tax deduction and thus reduce your tax bill. How much you'll save depends on your tax bracket.

Your Federal Tax Bracket	Amount of Tax Savings
15.0%	$300
28.0	560
31.0	620
36.0	720
39.6	792

Note: You may claim a full deduction—and reap the full amount of tax savings—if you're not covered by a pension or retirement plan at work. If you are covered, the amount of your deduction—and your tax savings—may be limited based on your adjusted gross income.

The Government Pays You to Save

Because of the tax savings, the single taxpayer's IRA contribution of $2,000 in our example really cost only $1,700, thanks to the tax saving of $300. For the married couple filing jointly, the true cost of making $4,000 in IRA contributions is only $3,400 because of the $600 savings in federal income tax.

It's not as if you lost the money, or spent it, or gambled it away. It's still your money. You just decided to put it in an account marked "IRA," where it will remain, and, it is hoped, will grow, until you need it. For this you get a tax break—one reason why the IRA can be such a good deal for you and why it can be better than putting your money in a taxable account, such as a bank account.

Another Tax Benefit

IRAs offer another big tax benefit: the money your IRA earns each year doesn't get taxed immediately. What's so special about that? Remember that with a bank account, as with lots of other types of taxable savings accounts, the interest you earn generally gets taxed every year. You report the interest on your tax return and you wind up paying taxes on it.

If you somehow forget to report your earned interest, you still get pinched because the bank sends a copy of your annual interest statement, Form 1099, not only to you but to the government too. If the IRS spots the discrepancy— and it usually does—you get a notice telling you to "fess up." You could also face interest and penalties.

Postponing the Tax Bill

IRAs don't work like traditional bank accounts. The money your IRA earns isn't taxed each year. Instead, the tax bill is postponed; it typically doesn't come due until you take your money out, which normally happens after you retire.

As a result, all the money that your IRA earns each year stays inside your IRA. This means that all of your money can continue to grow, not just the part of it that's left after the annual tax bite.

Experts refer to this deferred taxation as "the power of tax-deferred compounding." It means more money in your pocket. Here's how it works: Suppose you're paying tax at the federal rate of 15 percent, and you stash away $2,000 at the start of each year. Suppose, too, that your money earns 8 percent. If you put the money in a bank account or other taxable savings account, you'd have $85,678 after 20 years. But if you put your money in an IRA, you'd have $98,846 after 20 years.

Figure 3.2   Money Can Grow Faster in an IRA

If you contribute $2,000 a year to a traditional IRA and $2,000 to a regular taxable account, such as a bank account, your money will grow more quickly in the IRA because taxes are deferred

After Following Number of Years	Value of IRA	Value of Taxable Account
5	$ 11,733	$ 11,456
10	28,973	27,373
15	54,304	49,491
20	91,524	80,223
25	146,212	122,924
30	226,566	182,258

Note: The figures assume that $2,000 is contributed at the end of each year, both accounts grow at 8 percent a year, earnings in the taxable account are taxed each year, and the taxpayer is in the 15 percent federal income tax bracket. The higher the bracket, the smaller the amount in the taxable account.

More Money in Your Pocket

Simply by choosing an IRA as a place to save your money, you wind up with extra money—an extra $13,000 or so in our example above. When you have a taxable account, less money is available to grow because a part of your stockpile is leaking out to the tax man every year.

With an IRA, all your money is working for you, year-in, year-out. None of it trickles out of your account each year in taxes.

Our example above looked only at a 20-year time span. Over longer periods, the IRA advantage is even bigger. And if you're in a higher tax bracket, the advantage is greater still. (See Figure 3.2.)

More Time = More Savings

Let's say you're paying income tax at the 28 percent federal rate. You stash away $2,000 at the start of each year, and your money earns 8 percent a year. If you put the money in a bank account or a similar taxable savings account, you'd have $160,326 at the end of 30 years. But if you put your money in an IRA, you'd have $244,692 at the end of 30 years. In other words, by choosing an IRA as a place to save your money, you'd wind up with an extra $84,000 or so.

True, your IRA dollars are going to be taxed some day when they're withdrawn, but odds are you won't withdraw your IRA money in a lump sum.

You'll probably take out a little at a time to help meet expenses in retirement, and thus the rest of the money in your IRA will continue to grow, year after year, until it's withdrawn.

Why IRAs Make Sense

As you can see, then, IRAs have a lot going for them, which is one reason they're getting so much attention. And we're only talking here about the traditional deductible IRA; other, newer types of IRAs offer their own kinds of tax breaks.

The point is clear: the traditional IRA is an appealing way to save money for your retirement. And saving for retirement is important. Forget about all those debates about whether Social Security will still be around when you retire. Maybe it will, maybe it won't, or maybe it'll operate in a different way than it does today.

The real question is whether you'll have enough money to do the kinds of things you may want to do in retirement, whether you'll have some spare cash to help pay for such extras as traveling, dining out, going to shows, or attending to hobbies, things that add to the quality of your life.

How much you can do often depends on how much money you have. Social Security and pension benefits may take care of food, shelter, and your other basic needs, but having extra money stashed away in an IRA can add a lot of luster to your retirement years.

To Sum Up . . .

Tax benefits are what make IRAs so appealing. The federal government (and state government depending on where you live) is willing to help you save by giving you tax breaks for putting your money in a traditional IRA. You may get an immediate income tax deduction for contributing to an IRA, and the money in your account can grow each year without being taxed. If you take advantage, you can cash in on both these tax benefits—and watch your money really grow.

For More Information . . .

The Strong group of mutual funds has several free booklets that outline how IRAs work and how the new tax law affects IRAs. For information, write: Strong Funds, P.O. Box 2936, Milwaukee, WI 53201; or call 1-800-368-3863; or reach the company's Web site at www.strong-funds.com.

Do You Qualify for an IRA?

Who's eligible for the restyled classic IRA—and who isn't? Chapter 4 looks at the age and dollar limits on eligibility, why it's better to contribute money early instead of waiting until the deadline, why more people can now open traditional IRAs, and how IRAs offer a better deal for spouses.

Who gets to open an IRA? Just about everybody.

It doesn't matter if you have a pension plan at work. It doesn't matter if you work for somebody else or if you work for yourself. You can set aside money in an IRA for a given year as long as you have what the IRS calls "taxable compensation" or "earned income." (See Figure 4.1.)

Got a Job? Get an IRA

If you've got a job, you can set up an IRA and contribute money to it. And don't worry—the government uses a pretty broad definition of the word *job*. Basically, having a job means you made money either from wages, salary, tips, or commissions; and alimony counts too.

What doesn't count as job earnings are interest and dividend income, pensions and annuities, rental income, and items that you wouldn't normally consider income.

Dollar Limit

The bad news is that there are limits on IRAs. One is a dollar limit, which involves the amount you can contribute each year to an IRA.

The dollar limit is the same one you probably know by heart: $2,000. Technically, you can contribute a maximum of $2,000 or all of your taxable compensation, whichever is less. Refer again to Figure 4.1.

Figure 4.1   Can You Open an IRA?

Whether you can set up and contribute to a traditional IRA depends mainly on whether you have earned income, or what the government calls "taxable compensation."

What *is* taxable compensation:
- Wages
- Salaries
- Tips
- Professional fees
- Bonuses
- Commissions
- Self-employment income
- Alimony

What is *not* taxable compensation:
- Pension income
- Interest income
- Dividend income
- Rental income
- Social Security benefits
- Annuity income
- Deferred compensation
- Foreign earned income

Note: The IRS generally treats as compensation any amount listed in box 1 of your Form W-2. If you're self-employed, "compensation" means the net income from your trade or business reduced by your deduction for contributions on your behalf to retirement plans and by the deduction allowed for one-half of your self-employment taxes. "Alimony" means all taxable alimony and separate maintenance payments you receive under a decree. "Deferred compensation" means compensation payments postponed from a past year.
Source: Internal Revenue Service

In general, the government wants IRAs to be for working people. But if you earned only $1,000 from a job during a year, the most you can contribute to an IRA for that year is $1,000.

Age Limit

A second limit on IRAs is the contributor's age. You can set up and contribute to an IRA as long as you won't reach age 70½ by the end of the year. (If you've reached the age limit, you still have the right to transfer money from one IRA to another, but you can't make annual contributions.)

The good news is that you don't have to contribute to an IRA by the end of the tax year. You can wait until April 15 of the following year to make a contribution and it'll still be counted as having made a contribution for the previous year.

This little twist in the rules can come in handy. Suppose you couldn't scrape together enough money last year to make an IRA contribution, but you will have a little extra coming in during the first few months of this year. If that's the case, you have until April 15 of this year to make an IRA contribution and still have it count on your tax return for last year. The outfit that holds your IRA for you is generally known as your IRA trustee or custodian. You have to let your trustee or custodian know exactly what year the contribution is for. Remember to note this on your IRA form when making your contribution.

Watch the Deadline

Keep in mind, too, that April 15 is the final deadline for making IRA contributions for the previous year. If you plan to file your federal income tax return *after* April 15, you still must make your IRA contribution by April 15 to have it count for the prior year.

Of course, the earlier you make your IRA contribution, the better off you'll be because your money will have more time to grow. Even if you can't make the full $2,000 contribution at the start of each year, try to make smaller contributions regularly to your account throughout the year. Don't wait until the last minute if you can help it, because you will have missed the opportunity for your money to grow.

Suppose that starting in January, you can afford to set aside $167 at the beginning of each month, every month, for the year, and your money will grow at an annual rate of 8 percent. In this example, your account will be worth about $2,093, but if you wait until the end of the next year to make a full IRA contribution, your account will be worth only $2,000.

Early Contributions Pay Off

By contributing to your IRA in regular monthly installments throughout the year instead of making a lump sum contribution at the end of the year, you'll earn an extra $93 in the above example. For some people (like me!), $93 is a lot of money. Even if it's small potatoes to you, think about what that extra growth will do for your account year after year over lots and lots of years.

What if you don't have the time or the discipline to set aside money in an IRA each month? Let your IRA trustee or custodian do it for you. If you have a checking or similar account at your bank, most IRA trustees or custodians will supply you with the necessary forms to let them debit your bank account each month, making the contributions automatically for you. This can be a relatively painless way to save.

Save what you can afford.   Keep in mind, too, that you aren't required to make the full $2,000 contribution that's allowed for each year. If you've only got $500 to set aside, do it, and the earlier you can invest it, the better.

Remember that just about anybody can contribute to an IRA for a given year as long as the person has some type of earned income for the year. But will you be able to claim a federal income tax deduction for the amount you contribute to an IRA?

The Two-Part Test

Until Congress changed the rules in 1986, just about anyone who contributed to an IRA could claim a tax deduction. But with the Tax Reform Act of 1986, Congress clamped down. As a result of this 1986 law, anyone who wanted to claim a deduction for making an IRA contribution first had to pass a two-part test. Because the test was so strict, lots of taxpayers were no longer able to claim the deduction. And some who were eligible for an IRA deduction didn't bother with it because the two-part test seemed so complicated. As a result of Congress's crackdown, the national level of IRA contributions plunged.

Here's how the two-part test worked:

1. If you didn't have a pension plan at work (what the IRS calls an employer-sponsored "qualified plan"), then you could claim a federal income tax deduction for your IRA contribution. The amount you could deduct was equal to the amount you contribute to your IRA; thus, a $2,000 IRA contribution gave you a $2,000 deduction.
2. If you *did* take part in a pension plan at work (see Figure 4.2), the amount of the tax deduction you could claim generally depended on how much you earned.

This second part of the two-part test, the part that had to do with earnings, was tied to your adjusted gross income.

Figure 4.2   Are You Covered by a Pension?

Types of Employer-Sponsored Plans:

If you're not covered by a pension plan at work, you may claim a full federal income tax deduction for the amount you contribute to a traditional IRA. But if you *are* covered, the amount of your deduction depends on your income.

- Qualified pension, profit-sharing, stock bonus, money purchase, and Keogh plans
- 401(k) plans
- Union-sponsored plans
- Qualified annuity plans
- U.S. government pension or retirement plans
- 403(b) plans
- Simplified employee pension plans (SEPs)
- SIMPLE plans

When Are You Covered?

- For "Defined Contribution Plans" such as profit-sharing, stock bonus, and money purchase plans, you're considered covered if money is contributed or allocated to your account for the plan year that ends within your tax year.
- For "Defined Benefit Plans," which are traditional pension plans to which only the employer typically contributes, you're considered to be covered if you're eligible to participate for the plan year that ends within your tax year.

Note: In general, you're considered to be covered by an employer-sponsored plan if the "Pension Plan" box is checked on the Form W-2 Wage and Tax Statement you get from your employer. Coverage under Social Security or railroad retirement Tier I and Tier II benefits doesn't count as coverage under an employer-sponsored plan.
Source: Internal Revenue Service

Adjusted Gross Income and Your IRA Deduction

The line for your adjusted gross income is on the front of your federal income tax return toward the bottom. In general, it's your overall income reduced by some business expenses and certain other items. For the average taxpayer, adjusted gross income is just about the same as overall income. As a general rule, therefore, the more money you made from work each year under the 1986 law, the less likely you were to be eligible for an IRA deduction.

Here's how it worked:

- If you were single and your adjusted gross income was less than $25,000, you could claim a full deduction for your IRA contribution. If your adjusted gross income was between $25,000 and $35,000, you could deduct part of the money you contributed to an IRA. If your adjusted gross income was more than $35,000, you couldn't claim any federal income tax deduction for your IRA contribution.
- If you were married, filing jointly, and your adjusted gross income was less than $40,000, you could claim a full deduction; for adjusted gross income between $40,000 and $50,000, a partial deduction; for adjusted gross income above $50,000, no deduction.

Ineligibility from the Earnings Test

The dollar limits under the 1986 law had an instant and far-reaching impact. All single taxpayers who were covered by a pension plan at work and who had an adjusted gross income of more than $35,000 were no longer able to claim an IRA deduction. Likewise, all taxpayers who were married, filing jointly, and had an adjusted gross income of more than $50,000 could no longer claim an IRA deduction. And Congress gave no special treatment for married couples: If you were married, filing jointly, with adjusted gross income above $50,000 and *either* spouse was covered by a pension plan, then *neither* spouse could claim an IRA deduction.

It's clear, then, that the earnings test killed the IRA deduction for many taxpayers and dampened enthusiasm for IRAs overall. Worse still, Congress did not tie these dollar limits to inflation, so the limits remained fixed.

Congress Changes the Rules

It wasn't until 1997 that Congress finally changed the rules. The two-part test remained, but the limits were loosened. Congress still didn't tie the limits to inflation. Instead, the limits will rise according to a fixed schedule in the Taxpayer Relief Act of 1997, as shown in Figure 4.3.

Under the new law, the limits on deductions will generally increase each year through 2005 for single taxpayers and through 2007 for married couples filing jointly. For example:

- *Singles:* If you took part in a pension plan at work under the old rules, the only way you could get a full deduction for an IRA contribution was if your adjusted gross income was below $25,000 for 1997. But the

Figure 4.3   Is Your IRA Contribution Deductible?

To claim a federal income tax deduction for your IRA contribution, you must pass a two-part test. If you're not covered by a pension plan at work, your contribution is fully deductible. If you are covered by a pension plan at work, your ability to claim a deduction depends on your adjusted gross income (AGI).

For a Single Taxpayer

Year	AGI Phase-Out Range
1997	$25,000 to $35,000
1998	$30,000 to $40,000
1999	$31,000 to $41,000
2000	$32,000 to $42,000
2001	$33,000 to $43,000
2002	$34,000 to $44,000
2003	$40,000 to $50,000
2004	$45,000 to $55,000
2005 and after	$50,000 to $60,000

For Married Taxpayers Filing Jointly

Year	AGI Phase-Out Range
1997	$40,000 to $50,000
1998	$50,000 to $60,000
1999	$51,000 to $61,000
2000	$52,000 to $62,000
2001	$53,000 to $63,000
2002	$54,000 to $64,000
2003	$60,000 to $70,000
2004	$65,000 to $75,000
2005	$70,000 to $80,000
2006	$75,000 to $85,000
2007 and after	$80,000 to $100,000

Note: If your adjusted gross income is below the low end of the range for a given year, you may claim a full deduction for your IRA contribution; if your AGI falls within the range, a partial deduction; AGI above the range, no deduction. Separate rules apply for someone who is not covered by a pension plan but whose spouse is covered.
Source: U.S. Congress

new law boosted the limit to $30,000 for 1998. It'll keep rising year after year until it reaches $50,000 for 2005. (For purposes of this test, the word *single* means that the filing status on your federal income tax return is either "single" or "head of household.")

- *Married, Filing Jointly:* Under the 1986 rules, if either you or your spouse took part in a pension plan at work, neither of you could claim a full deduction for an IRA contribution unless your adjusted gross income was under $40,000 for 1997. Under the new law, this limit was boosted to $50,000 for 1998 and keeps rising year after year until it reaches $80,000 in 2007. In other words, for married couples covered by a pension plan who file a joint federal income tax return, the limit *doubles* in ten years. (For purposes of this test, the phrase "married filing jointly" means that the filing status on your federal income tax return is either "married filing jointly" or "qualifying widow or widower.")

Remember: Technically, you don't use your adjusted gross income to figure the tax deduction you may claim. You have to use what is called your "modified adjusted gross income." In general, your modified adjusted gross income is simply your adjusted gross income *before* you deduct your IRA contribution as well as any amount you might normally exclude from income for the Series EE U.S. savings bond education plan, any foreign earned income you may have had, and any foreign housing exclusion or deduction you might claim. As a general rule, your modified adjusted gross income will be the same as your adjusted gross income.

Opening the Door

Maybe there's far more detail here than you really need to know. But think about the impact of the new law. As each year passes, more and more taxpayers will be able to claim at least a partial deduction—if not a *full* deduction—for contributions they make to IRAs.

In other words, by increasing the dollar limits, Congress made traditional IRAs a lot more attractive to a lot more people. If you can get an income tax deduction for contributing to an IRA, then IRAs should look a lot better to you, especially when compared with other investments that don't allow you a deduction.

What if your income falls between the limits? How much of a federal income tax deduction will you get by contributing to an IRA? To figure it out, you don't need a calculator and you don't need a computer. You can use a handy little formula to get the answer, and all you really need is a pencil and piece of paper.

Figuring Your IRA Deduction: A Handy Formula

Let's see how to figure your IRA deduction.

Figure 4.3 in this chapter shows two columns of figures, one for singles and one for married couples filing jointly.

From one of the columns, pick a year. You'll see that the year includes a dollar range.

- If your adjusted gross income is below the range, you can claim a full deduction for your IRA contribution.
- If it's above the range, you can't claim a deduction.
- If it's within the range, you can claim a partial deduction on your income tax return.

To see how much of a deduction you'll get, subtract your adjusted gross income from the high end of the range. Multiply the result by 0.20, which is how much of a deduction you'll get.

Sound hard? It really isn't. These two examples may help:

1. Maria is single, will have an adjusted gross income of $35,000 for the 1998 tax year, and is covered by a pension plan at work. According to Figure 4.3, the dollar range for that year is $30,000 to $40,000. The high end of that dollar range, then, is $40,000. She will subtract her adjusted gross income ($35,000) from the high end of the dollar range ($40,000). The result is $5,000. Next, she multiplies $5,000 by .20. (In other words, 20 percent of $5,000.) The answer in this example is $1,000, so Maria may contribute the full $2,000 for the year, but she'll be able to claim a $1,000 deduction on her federal income tax return.
2. Joe and Lucy are married and filing a joint income tax return for the 1999 tax year. Both have jobs and both are covered by pension plans at work. Their adjusted gross income is $53,000. Figure 4.3 shows that the dollar range for 1999 is $51,000 to $61,000, so the high end of that dollar range for 1999 is $61,000. When Joe and Lucy subtract $53,000 from $61,000, the result is $8,000. They multiply that by .20. (In other words, 20 percent of $8,000.) The result is $1,600. Thus, if they each contribute $2,000 to an IRA, they each can claim a $1,600 federal income tax deduction for 1999.

Nonworking spouse. If you're married, file a joint tax return, and either you or your spouse doesn't have a job, there's another big change in the rules that you probably can use to your advantage.

Under the old rules, if either you or your spouse took part in a pension plan at work, neither of you could claim a deduction for IRA contributions unless your income fell within or below certain dollar limits. This was especially painful if your spouse worked but you didn't. In effect, the working spouse who took part in an employer-sponsored pension plan "tainted" the nonworking spouse.

Congress has changed that rule. Now you won't be considered a so-called active participant in an employer-sponsored pension plan just because your spouse is if you don't work. But here, too, Congress has imposed dollar limits. If your adjusted gross income is below $150,000 for the year, there's no problem in claiming an IRA deduction. If your adjusted gross income is between $150,000 and $160,000, the deduction gets reduced, or "phased out"; above $160,000, no deduction is allowed.

To show how the limits work, here are two examples based on a report by a congressional committee on the 1997 tax law:

1. Suppose that Walter takes part in a pension plan sponsored by his company. His wife, Thelma, isn't employed; she stays at home, raising their children. The couple's adjusted gross income for the year is $200,000. In this case, both Walter and Thelma can contribute to IRAs, but neither can claim a deduction because their adjusted gross income is higher than the limit.
2. Assume the same facts as above except that Walter and Thelma's adjusted gross income is $125,000. Here again both Walter and Thelma can contribute to IRAs. But the result is different: Walter's contribution isn't deductible because he doesn't meet the income limits for people who are active participants in an employer-sponsored plan. But Thelma's contribution *is* deductible—fully deductible, in fact— because the couple's income is below the special limits ($150,000 to $160,000) that applies to couples whose working spouse is in a pension plan but the nonworking spouse is not.

You can see the impact of this change: the average homemaker—whether male or female—is now able to claim a full deduction for his or her IRA contribution. In other words, whether a homemaker's IRA contribution is deductible is no longer tied to whether the working spouse takes part in an employer-sponsored pension plan.

To Sum Up . . .

Just about anyone can open a traditional IRA today. All you really need is earned income—which you get from holding a job. Although you still must pass a two-part test to see if you can claim a federal income tax deduction for the money you contribute to an IRA, the dollar limits in the test are higher now and will continue to rise as the years pass. As a result, more and more people will be eligible to get the deduction—a valuable tax break. If you can afford to contribute, do so. And keep in mind that the rules have been relaxed for nonworking spouses.

For More Information . . .

This chapter includes examples that show how you might be able to claim a federal income tax deduction for the money you contribute to a regular IRA. To get a better idea, check out the worksheets and detailed instructions that the IRS provides in Publication 590, *Individual Retirement Arrangements*. For a free copy of this booklet, you can call the IRS at 1-800-TAX-FORM (1-800-829-3676). You also can get a copy by completing the order form in your Form 1040 tax package. If you have access to a computer, you can get a copy by contacting the IRS's Web site at www.irs.ustreas.gov.

Where to Invest Your IRA Dollars

Chapter 5 examines how—and where—to open an IRA. It reviews IRA choices and how they compare—banks, mutual fund companies, stock brokerages, or stock-issuing companies—as well as some new choices for IRA investors and how to get the best returns on your investment.

So now you've decided to open an IRA. Congratulations! What's next? You have to decide where to put it.

You can't just hide your IRA in a mattress. Somebody has to hold your IRA for you in safekeeping, in trust, because it is technically a trust, or custodial, account set up for either your benefit or the benefit of yourself and your beneficiary.

A third party, usually a bank or some other financial institution, has to serve as your IRA's trustee or custodian. It's the trustee's or custodian's job to make sure all the paperwork is in order, that the account meets all the rules, and that all the right forms get filed and reported to the IRS at the right time.

An Outline of Your Rights

Your trustee or custodian *must* give you a copy of a written document that outlines the rules for your account and its terms and conditions at about the time you set up the account. The document must show that your account meets all these requirements:

- Your account's trustee or custodian must be either a bank, a federally insured credit union, a savings and loan association (also known as an S&L, thrift, or savings bank), or some other outfit—such as a mutual fund company or insurance company—that has the IRS's stamp of approval to act as trustee or custodian.

- The trustee or custodian can't accept contributions of more than $2,000 a year to an IRA on your behalf. (This annual dollar limit is higher if you're transferring—or rolling over—money from another IRA or from certain types of pension plans at work. More on rollovers later.)
- You can only use cash, not property or other assets, to open an IRA. (For rollovers, other rules apply.)
- The written document describing the terms and conditions of your IRA must show that you always have the right to withdraw all your money if you want to. (As the experts would say, your account must be "fully vested" at all times. In other words, you have a so-called nonforfeitable right to withdraw everything that's in the account at any time.)
- In general, your IRA trustee or custodian can't mingle your account with other accounts; your IRA is yours, and the assets contained in your account generally must be kept separate from other accounts. (One exception: mutual funds.)
- Your trustee or custodian generally must see to it that you begin to make withdrawals from your IRA by April 1 of the year following the year in which you reach age 70½. (There are some exceptions.)

All these things are important, of course, but if you're just starting out, they are really just technical points. Most or all of them will be spelled out in the paperwork that you get when you open your account. You generally don't have to fret over these issues; the outfit that serves as your IRA trustee or custodian will notify you from time to time, usually by mail, about any technical matters you should know that involve your account.

Where to Open an Account

Once you've chosen to open an IRA, your biggest decisions—and your only ones—are where to open the account and to invest the money in the account. In other words, who's going to get your business?

Fortunately, you have a lot of options, which is one reason IRAs are so popular. With some other types of retirement savings plans, such as 401(k) and 403(b) plans at work, your investment options may be limited. In some cases, your investment choices are restricted to just a few mutual funds or a few insurance companies, for example.

IRAs, on the other hand, typically offer you a lot more flexibility. Some people open IRAs at their local bank or credit union, mainly for convenience and perhaps out of a concern for safety. There's nothing wrong with that. Maybe your life is too busy and too complicated, and you don't have a lot of time or energy to check out all the options. Or maybe you're just sick of having to make so many choices in your life each day. You want to open an IRA, put your money in a safe place, and forget about it.

That's okay. Just keep in mind that there are more places to open an IRA than banks, thrifts, and credit unions, and some of these other options may suit you better.

Safety in Federal Insurance

By sticking your IRA dollars in a federally insured account at a bank, thrift, or credit union, you can be certain that your principal is safe so long as the money in your account falls within federal insurance limits (generally $100,000 per depositor per account).

If you figure you'll need to use the money in a fairly short time—to help pay a college tuition bill, buy your first house, or cover expenses in retirement, for example—then a federally insured bank account is a sound choice. Don't trouble yourself with any other worries. Just get the job done.

Small Returns

Don't expect big returns, though. Federally insured accounts offer safety of principal but not much in the way of returns. These accounts generally pay you interest at about the same rate you'd get from a non-IRA account. If your bank is offering 5 percent interest on a short-term certificate of deposit, for example, the bank will probably offer you about the same rate of interest on a short-term IRA. Longer-term IRAs usually yield about the same as longer-term CDs.

Sure, some banks pay more than others. If you shop around, you might find a better deal at an out-of-state bank, or at an in-state bank that might be trying to boost its business. No matter where you finally wind up, the interest that's paid on federally insured accounts at banks, thrifts, and credit unions has been, at least in recent years, only a little higher than the rate of inflation.

Yes, your money will grow. And the longer you keep it in your account, the more it will grow. But will it grow enough to give you the kind of nest egg you're hoping to build for your retirement? Might other places give you a better return in the long run and a bigger pile of cash when it comes time to retire?

Your Investment Options

You can invest your IRA dollars in a mutual fund, for example, or in stocks or bonds. History shows that over the long haul these investments are far more likely to outpace inflation than a typical bank account would, so you could wind up with a lot more money in the end.

To get the higher returns, however, you have to be willing to assume some risk. And that's the trade-off. The value of stocks or of shares in a stock mutual fund, for example, can rise or fall over time, depending on market conditions and other factors. You may profit or you may lose money—an important point to remember. For much of the 1980s and 1990s, the stock market soared. Some investors, especially those who were new to the market, began to assume that this is how the stock market always operates: It goes up and keeps going up; the value of your investments rises, and everybody's happy.

Remember the 1970s?   In the mid-1970s, the stock market tumbled as inflation heated up and the nation was battered by oil shocks. The stock market plunged, losing nearly half its value; it took five years or more (depending on how you measure it) for the overall market to recover. That's a long time to wait.

If a market tumble happened again, would you worry? Would you hold on until the rebound? Or would you lose heart, cash out, and lock in losses? For much of the 1990s the stock market boomed, but not all stocks—and not all stock mutual funds—shared fully in the rally.

Before you make a choice about where to put your IRA and how to invest your IRA dollars, you've got to search your soul. Figure out whether you can stomach the ups and downs, and decide whether the constant drumbeat of news about individual stocks and mutual funds, and about the market as a whole, would keep you awake at night with worry.

In other words, you've got to figure out how well, or how poorly, you tolerate risk. If you don't like risk, stick your money in a bank account and sleep tight. But if you can stomach some risk, if you can hang in there through the roller-coaster ride, if you've got the time and if you've got the patience, the rewards of investing in stocks (and stock mutual funds) can be enormous.

Risk and Return from Stocks

Put $2,000 today in a bank account that earns an average of 5 percent a year over 20 years. In the end, you'll have stockpiled about $5,300 (before accounting for taxes). Not bad. But if you put $2,000 today in a stock mutual fund that earns an average of 10 percent a year over 20 years, you'll have about $13,450 in the end. In other words, the stock mutual fund in this example would have given you about $8,150 *more* than you would have gotten from the bank account.

Is this comparison fair? In some ways, it isn't. Not every stock or stock mutual fund will generate a good annual return for you. But as a general rule, stocks and stock mutual funds will give you a better return over long periods of time than you'd normally get from a bank account.

Still, only you can decide if you have the patience to ride out the stock market's storms in the meantime; a mutual fund, stockbroker, or financial adviser can't do it for you.

Mutual Funds

If you decide to press ahead, your choices are practically unlimited. There are thousands of mutual funds from which to choose and thousands more individual stocks. And there are lots of ways that an IRA investor can take advantage.

You can choose an investment company to hold your IRA, for example. Investment companies pool people's money and use it to buy things such as stocks and bonds. These investment pools are known as mutual funds, and they're a popular place for IRAs.

How popular are mutual funds? The numbers tell the story: In 1981 about $26 billion was invested in IRAs, but only about 10 percent of those IRA dollars were in mutual funds. By 1996, however, the amount of money invested in IRAs had swollen to about $1.35 trillion, according to the Investment Company Institute in Washington. And about 51 percent of those IRA dollars were in mutual funds, as shown in Figure 5.1. In other words, by the end of 1996, mutual fund IRAs held well over $600 billion in assets, and the number of accounts holding IRAs had soared, too.

Professional Management and Diversification

Why are mutual funds so popular? Many investors like mutual funds because they offer what the experts call "professional management and diversification."

In other words, mutual funds typically hire professional money managers and support staff to manage the money that comes from you and thousands of other investors like you. And by pooling investors' money, mutual funds can invest in a much wider variety of stocks and other securities than an individual investor could afford to do alone.

Figure 5.1   Mutual Fund IRAs (in millions of accounts)

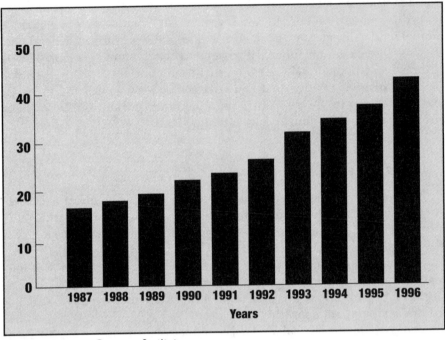

Source: Investment Company Institute

How do you go about picking a mutual fund that's right for you? Today it's easy. Most major newspapers offer lots of stories about mutual funds, usually in their business section.

How to Pick a Mutual Fund

Magazines such as *Money, Kiplinger's,* and *Consumer Reports* also focus a lot of attention on mutual funds. Libraries and bookstores are packed with all sorts of books about mutual funds. And to help in your selection, the reference section in your local public library probably keeps on file some guides—such as Morningstar and the Value Line Mutual Fund Survey—that are designed especially to help small investors choose and keep track of mutual funds. There's a ton of information; all you have to do is a little research, often at little or no expense.

Most of these reference tools will give you detailed information on each fund, including how it has performed, how much money you need to invest up front, and how to contact the fund.

Many funds are sold directly to investors; you just call the fund, usually through a toll-free number, and you'll receive an application form along with the fund's official offering document, known as a "prospectus." The prospectus outlines all the details you need to know about what the fund is, how it works, its potential risks and rewards, and other information.

After you read the prospectus, you mail back your completed application form, along with a check, and you're all set. The fund keeps you informed with regular mailings and typically will send you an account statement quarterly, monthly, or whenever there's a transaction involving your account. Many funds also let you set up an automatic investment plan under which a fund takes a certain amount out of your bank account automatically at regular intervals, usually monthly. In this way, you don't have to plunk down your money all at once; you invest a little at a time.

Picking a Stock Brokerage

You may also open an IRA with a securities brokerage. And here, too, there are lots of options. A quick look at some of the main ones:

- Big stock brokerages, usually called "full-service" brokers, such as Merrill Lynch, PaineWebber, or Smith Barney, have local offices throughout the country that offer lots of services, including professional advice. In exchange, you generally pay full price for the services.
- Discount brokers, such as Charles Schwab & Co. or Jack White & Co., typically have fewer offices, offer somewhat fewer services, and provide less in the way of professional advice, but their fees and other charges are usually somewhat less too.
- So-called deep-discount brokerages usually operate few offices and do most of their business over the phone. They generally offer less in services and advice, but their fees are typically less than either the full-service brokerages or the discounters.

Magazines and other periodicals, such as the journal published by the American Association of Individual Investors in Chicago, publish articles once a year or more that compare brokerages by fees, services, and other standards.

Self-Directed Accounts

Through a broker, you can set up an IRA and invest in mutual funds, for example. But brokerages offer another option: you can set up what's known as a "self-directed IRA."

With this type of IRA, you're the quarterback. Instead of letting a mutual fund's portfolio manager decide how to invest your money, *you* decide. You tell the broker exactly how your IRA dollars are to be invested. You can pick individual stocks, bonds, or other securities. You can sell some or all of the securities in your account when you want and buy others. The broker typically charges some sort of fee for each transaction within your self-directed IRA, but this type of account also offers maximum flexibility for the do-it-yourself investor.

Keep in mind that there are fewer and fewer differences between banks, brokerages, and mutual fund companies as time goes on. Banks are buying brokerages, for example; brokerages are getting more into the banking business; and your mutual fund company may turn out to be a subsidiary of a giant holding company that also owns banks and brokerages.

Depending on where you live, you might be able to walk into the lobby of your local bank and open a federally insured IRA at a teller window, or open a mutual fund IRA or a self-directed IRA by visiting the investment specialist who's sitting on the other side of the room. These options may also be offered through the brokerage you've chosen or through the mutual fund company you've picked.

More Options

Had enough? There's more. If you have a computer, there are plenty of ways to open an IRA online. Many brokerages and mutual fund companies have affiliates or subsidiaries that conduct business on the Internet. Some deep, deep discount brokerages operate exclusively on the Internet, allowing you to invest in mutual funds, stocks, or other securities, sometimes for only pennies a share. (Just make sure your transactions are secure.)

Don't forget that insurance companies also offer IRAs. If you're already doing business with an insurance agent, your agent probably has lots of computer software available not only to help calculate how much life insurance you'll need, for example, but also to figure out your retirement funding needs. It can be fairly simple for your agent to add an IRA to your portfolio of insurance and investment tools. And if you do business directly with an insurance company, such as USAA Life in Texas, you may also set up an IRA with relative ease.

Investing Directly in Stocks

Do-it-yourself investors can also open IRAs with a growing number of companies that sell stock directly to investors.

Figure 5.2   Dividend Reinvestment Plans

These companies offer either dividend reinvestment plans, direct-share purchase plans, or both. These plans also feature an IRA option, whereby, in effect, the companies sponsor your IRA and your IRA holds the stock.

Ameritech
30 S. Wacker Dr.
Chicago, IL 60606
Phone: 1-800-233-1342

Atmos Energy
P.O. Box 650205
Dallas, TX 75265-0205
Phone: 1-800-38-ATMOS

Bell Atlantic
1717 Arch St.
Philadelphia, PA 19103-2787
Phone: 1-800-631-2355

Exxon
5959 Las Clinas Blvd.
Irving, TX 75039-2298
Phone: 1-800-252-1800

Lucent Technologies
600 Mountain Rd.
Murray Hill, NJ 07974
Phone: 1-888-582-3686

McDonald's
McDonald's Plaza
Oak Brook, IL 60521-2278
Phone: 1-800-621-7825

Mobil
c/o Chase/Mellon Shareholder
   Services
P.O. Box 750
Pittsburgh, PA 15230
Phone: 1-800-648-9291

Morton International
c/o First Chicago Trust Co.
P.O. Box 2598
Jersey City, NJ 07303-2598
Phone: 1-800-990-1010

OGE Energy
P.O. Box 321
Oklahoma City, OK 73101-0321
Phone: 1-800-395-2662

Philadelphia Suburban
762 Lancaster Ave.
Bryn Mawr, PA 19010-3489
Phone: 1-800-205-8314

Sears, Roebuck
c/o First Chicago Trust Co.
P.O. Box 2598
Jersey City, NJ 07303-2598
Phone: 1-888-732-7788

UtiliCorp
P.O. Box 13287
Kansas City, MO 64199-3287
Phone: 1-800-487-6661

Note: Some companies may charge annual account maintenance, administration, or service fees and may levy charges for buying or selling shares. Phone numbers and addresses may be for the company itself or for its bank or other agent. Some plans may not be available in all states. (Information on many of these and other companies is available from the No-Load Stock Clearinghouse, 1-800-774-4117.)
Source: *Directory of Companies Offering Dividend Reinvestment Plans* (Evergreen Enterprises: Laurel, Maryland)

Here's how it works. Although most companies use brokers or other middlemen to sell stock to investors, more and more companies are establishing direct share-purchase plans, also called "no-load stock" programs.

These plans let you buy your first share—and every share—directly from the company itself, often for little or nothing in transaction costs. This lets you bypass brokerages, which can save you money on commissions and other fees.

And a small but growing number of these companies will let you set up an IRA with them, or their agent; they'll hold the shares that you buy directly.

Lots of companies also offer dividend reinvestment plans, or DRIPs, as shown in Figure 5.2. If you own stock in these companies, you can use the dividends the companies pay you to buy more stock automatically instead of taking the dividends in the form of cash. (Some companies that have direct purchase stock plans also offer DRIPs; others don't have direct purchase stock plans but do offer DRIPs—and some of these DRIP plans also include an IRA feature.)

Even More Investment Choices

The 1997 tax law that radically changed the rules for IRAs also gives you more choices for exactly what your IRA dollars can buy. Are you fond of gold or other precious metals? The law now lets you invest your IRA dollars in platinum coins or in silver, gold, platinum, or palladium bullion (as long as the precious metal is physically held by your IRA trustee, not by you). If you're interested, a bank or brokerage might be willing to serve as trustee or custodian for the precious metals in your IRA.

No matter which of all these options you choose, and no matter which outfit you pick to hold your IRA, remember that you've got to do some research first. Once you've decided to go beyond a bank, thrift, or credit union, and once you've compared the various fees and other expenses involved, there are risks to consider and investment choices that you should—and should not—make.

The price of precious metals can bounce around a lot. The price of gold, for example, soared in the early 1980s but then slumped. Are you sure you want your retirement money invested in gold or other precious metals?

Keep in mind, too, that no matter what type of IRA you choose, the money inside your IRA is going to grow without any immediate tax consequences. It generally makes no sense therefore to plunk your IRA dollars into such investments as U.S. Treasury securities, municipal bonds, or mutual funds that invest in government bonds.

IRAs Don't Stand Alone

If you wind up opening an IRA or if you already have one, please keep in mind a point that's worth repeating over and over: When it comes time to choose where to put your IRA dollars, remember that your IRA doesn't stand alone; it's part of your overall financial picture. When you're picking investments for your IRA, give some thought to where the rest of your money is invested because your IRA is part of your overall financial plan.

As an example, suppose you've got some sort of retirement savings plan at work that lets you choose how the money is to be invested, such as a 401(k), 403(b), or 457 plan, and all the money is invested in stock mutual funds.

Suppose, too, that you own some stock mutual funds directly that are not connected with your workplace. And let's also say that you keep your spare cash to a minimum; you prefer to put all your money in mutual funds.

When it comes time to decide how to invest your IRA dollars, you certainly do *not* want them invested in stocks or stock mutual funds in this example. Why? Because too many of your assets are already tied to the fate of the stock market. And one of the keys to successful investing is to spread your money around and not have all or most of it concentrated in just one area.

Like your mother or grandmother probably once told you, don't put all your eggs in one basket. The same is true for investments. Spread your assets among different types of investments, including stocks (and stock mutual funds); bonds (and bond mutual funds); and cash (or things that can be quickly converted to cash, such as money market mutual funds, short-term U.S. Treasury securities, Series EE U.S. savings bonds, and short-term bond mutual funds).

In the example above, you probably have too much in stocks already, so you can use your IRA as a starting point to diversify your investment portfolio. Instead of investing your IRA dollars in stocks or stock mutual funds, you might put them in bond funds, for instance.

The Importance of Your Time Horizon

Another key point: If you've looked carefully at your overall investment picture and you think your IRA dollars should be invested in stocks or stock mutual funds, consider your time horizon first.

In other words, remember what happened to stocks in the mid-1970s when the market lost nearly half its value? When stocks not only went down but *stayed down* for about five years on average?

Suppose the 1970 stock tumble were to happen again. Suppose, too, that your IRA dollars were invested in stocks or stock mutual funds. And suppose you had to withdraw some or all of your money from your IRA. How much would you get? Maybe not as much as you had planned on. Maybe even not as much as you had originally contributed because the value of the stock market had declined so much.

The point is this: If you've got a long-term time horizon, if you won't need to tap your IRA for another 10, 20, or 30 years or longer, then stocks and stock mutual funds can be a sound investment choice. Odds are you'll have plenty of time to ride out the market's ups and downs in the meantime.

If you have a shorter time horizon, however, then stocks and stock mutual funds probably aren't the place to invest your IRA dollars. If retirement is just a couple of years around the corner, for instance, and you'll need to withdraw some or all of your IRA money at that time to help meet expenses, you'll probably want to put most or all of your IRA dollars into something conservative and safe, such as a federally insured bank account, so you'll know the money will be there when you need it. The same holds true if you're planning to use some or all of your IRA dollars within a few years to help buy a house or pay for a child's college education.

As the old saying goes, sometimes the return *of* your principal is more important than the return *on* your principal.

To Sum Up . . .

IRAs are flexible. Lots of places will hold your account for you. If you want to play it safe, stick with a bank, thrift, or credit union. Most of them offer federal deposit insurance, so you know your money will be protected as long as you keep within the insurance limits.

If you want a better return on your investment—you want your money to grow more over the long run—then stocks are the place to be. There are lots of ways to invest in stocks—through mutual fund companies, through securities brokerages, or through certain types of insurance company products. You can also invest your IRA dollars directly in certain companies.

Just remember that with the higher potential returns that stocks and stock mutual funds may offer come higher risks. You can cope with the higher level of risk by investing only for the long run, so you can ride out any market downturns in the meantime. But if your time horizon is short—if you'll need your money within a few years—keep away from the stock market and play it safe with conservative investments.

For More Information . . .

- The Investment Company Institute in Washington, a trade group for the mutual fund industry, publishes a comprehensive list of thousands of mutual funds. Its annual directory includes the name, address, and phone number for each fund. The directory is available for under $10. The institute also publishes free brochures about the basics of mutual fund investing. For order information, write: Investment Company Institute, 1401 H St. N.W., Suite 1200, Washington, DC 20005-2148.

  The institute also offers some booklets about investing that you may get free of charge by writing to the address above. These include *A Guide to Mutual Funds* available in either English or Spanish; *A Guide to Closed-End Funds* also in either English or Spanish; and *A Guide to Unit Investment Trusts* available in either English or Spanish.

  If you have access to a computer, you can get more information from the institute's Web site at www.ici.org.
- The Mutual Fund Education Alliance, a nonprofit group for mutual funds that are sold directly to the public, also publishes guides and booklets about funds and fund investing. Its Web site has tools to help you learn about, choose, and monitor mutual funds. It also features links to mutual funds that have their own Web sites, and it has a section you can use to set up and keep track of your own portfolio of funds. Here's the address: www.mfea.com.
- The American Association of Individual Investors (AAII) is a nonprofit group that has local chapters throughout the country to help people learn more about investing. You can join one of the chapters or just belong to the national organization. The annual membership fee, about $40, includes a subscription to the *AAII Journal*, a magazine that accepts no advertising and is packed with articles, charts, and tables for the individual investor, including detailed comparisons of fees charged by discount brokerages. For information, write: AAII, 625 N. Michigan Ave., Chicago, IL 60611. You can also get information at the group's Web site: www.aaii.com.
- For information on how to order a directory of companies that offer dividend reinvestment plans, write: Evergreen Enterprises, P.O. Box 763, Laurel, MD 20725.
- For a free copy of the *No-Load Stock Insider* newsletter, which includes a master list of companies that offer no-load stock plans, write: No-Load Stock Insider, 7412 Calumet Ave., Suite 200, Hammond, IN 46324. For more on no-load stocks (and dividend reinvestment plans), here are two related Web sites: www.dripinvestor.com and www.no load stocks.com.

Managing Your IRA

This chapter explains how to reduce or avoid annual maintenance fees (or claim an income tax deduction if you pay a fee); how to transfer or roll over money from one traditional IRA to another; and when moving money from a pension plan to a traditional IRA is—and isn't—a good idea.

There was a time not long ago that IRA trustees and custodians were happy just to have your business. You'd open an account, deposit some cash, and that would be that.

The bank, credit union, brokerage, or mutual fund that you chose to hold your IRA would invest your IRA dollars on your behalf and then take a little bit off the top to cover expenses and earn a profit. But trustees and custodians complained that IRAs required too much paperwork to make the accounts profitable enough. So they started charging fees.

Avoiding Fees

Assessing fees for IRA accounts began with just a few custodians and trustees, but it soon became pretty much industrywide practice. To boost profitability, IRA clients were charged $10 or $15 or $20 a year in annual fees.

Call them "custodial" fees, "maintenance" fees, "administrative" fees, or whatever other fancy name you want. The bottom line is that IRA owners might be saving money in taxes each year, but they were getting whacked with fees.

For wealthy people with lots of money to invest, the fees were nothing but a small annoyance, a cost of doing business. But for the small or average investor, the fees could take a big bite out of annual earnings.

How Fees Reduce Your Return

Suppose, for instance, that you invest the annual limit, $2,000, in an IRA at the start of the year. The account grows by 8 percent so that one year later your IRA is worth $2,160, which represents $2,000 from your original contribution plus $160 in earnings.

Now suppose your account's custodian or trustee hits you with a $20 annual account maintenance fee. Suddenly, you've earned $140 for the year, not $160. And your percentage gain for the year is now down to 7 percent, not 8 percent. In other words, in this example the annual fee has eaten one full percentage point out of your earnings. Ouch!

You probably have the option to pay the fee out-of-pocket so that it isn't subtracted from the money inside your account. This lets more of your money remain in your account to grow tax deferred through the years. Still, it's money you must pay whether it comes out of your account or out of your pocket.

Most Fees Don't Qualify for a Deduction

An annual IRA fee that you pay out-of-pocket can generally be claimed as a deduction from your federal income tax—but only if you itemize your deductions. But most taxpayers don't itemize because they haven't enough expenses to qualify; they're stuck with the standard one-size-fits-all deduction.

Even if you do itemize, there's a chance you may miss out on claiming a tax benefit for your IRA custodial fee because the annual IRA fee falls under a category of expenses known as "miscellaneous" itemized deductions.

A miscellaneous deductible item can be claimed as a deduction only to the extent that your IRA fee and other similar expenses exceed 2 percent of your adjusted gross income. Thus, you have to lump the IRA fee together with a grab bag of other expenses, including the amount you pay for union dues, professional dues, and certain educational expenses as well as magazines, newspapers, and books offering investment advice (including this book!) and enter the total on Schedule A of your federal income tax return. But you get to deduct only that part of all your miscellaneous deductions that amounts to more than 2 percent of your adjusted gross income.

A Limit on Deductions

If you had $30,000 in adjusted gross income but only $500 in miscellaneous itemized deductions, you couldn't claim any of these deductions. If they totaled $650 in this example, you could claim only $50. In the end, then, paying the annual IRA fee out-of-pocket may not give you a tax benefit at all. What to do?

Lots of IRA owners have long complained about IRA fees. And the financial services industry has listened. As a result, some brokerages, such as Charles Schwab, have generally agreed to waive annual IRA fees altogether if the value of an IRA exceeds a certain amount (typically $10,000). Some mutual fund companies, including Scudder and the mutual fund family operated under the umbrella of the American Association of Retired Persons, have generally waived annual IRA fees altogether. If fees bother you like they bother me, you can save money by shopping around.

IRAs are flexible enough so that you can move your money from one IRA custodian or trustee to another with relatively few problems and no tax consequences. The two ways to move your IRA are discussed in the following sections and shown in Figure 6.1.

Transferring Your IRA

You can transfer your IRA from one trustee or custodian to another directly with no tax impact. The Internal Revenue Service allows an unlimited number of such direct transfers each year, so if you're fed up with one trustee or custodian, you can transfer your account without paying income tax or a penalty.

What's more, some outfits will handle the transfer for you at no charge. You just contact the new IRA custodian or trustee, complete the application, and turn it in. The new custodian or trustee will then arrange to have your account transferred, directly and automatically, with no additional steps required by you.

Just remember that the process may take some time. Your old trustee or custodian may not be pleased to lose your account and may not make the transfer a top priority. Keep in mind, too, that your old IRA custodian or trustee may charge a fee for closing your account. Some brokerages, for example, levy stiff account-closing fees. To see if you'll be liable and find out how much you may be charged, check the language in your original account contract.

Rolling Over Your IRA

Another way to move money or other assets from one IRA to another tax-free is through a rollover. In effect, you act as the go-between, the middleman.

Figure 6.1   IRA Transfers and Rollovers

You may move money from one IRA to another, from a retirement plan to an IRA, or from an IRA to a retirement plan. Here's a summary of the types of transfers and rollovers available:

Transfers

- A transfer generally refers to the direct movement of money from one IRA trustee or custodian to another. The dollars (or other plan assets) aren't paid out or distributed to you; they're transferred directly, behind the scenes, from one IRA to another.
- Transfers require no withholding and do not result in tax consequences.
- You may have an unlimited number of transfers in any given year.

Rollovers

Rollovers require a payout, or distribution, of money to you. You then have 60 days to move that money to another IRA or a company-sponsored retirement plan.

- If you fail to complete the rollover in time, the amount of the payout is generally subject to federal income tax and may face a 10 percent early withdrawal penalty.
- You're generally allowed one rollover in every 12-month period.
- Investors sometimes use a rollover to get temporary access to their funds. It lets you make a short-term loan to yourself with no tax consequences as long as you replace the money within the 60-day deadline.
- If you use a regular rollover for a distribution of money from a company-sponsored pension or retirement plan, the company must withhold 20 percent of it even if you planned to roll over the entire amount (see "Direct Rollovers" below). This can have complex tax consequences.

Figure 6.1   IRA Transfers and Rollovers (Continued)

Direct Rollovers

- To avoid the withholding requirement of a rollover from a company pension or retirement plan, you may choose a direct rollover. In a direct rollover, the money is transferred directly from the company plan to an IRA or to a pension or retirement plan at another company; no tax consequences result.
- If you plan to use an IRA as a temporary parking place for money from a direct rollover, use a "conduit IRA." This preserves some of the tax benefits of an employer-sponsored plan and lets you move the money later to a pension or retirement plan at another job.
- You can't use a direct rollover for after-tax contributions you made to your employer-sponsored retirement or pension plan. You also can't use it to transfer money you must accept as part of a required minimum withdrawal.

As with a transfer, you can roll over some or all of the money (or other assets) from one IRA to the other.

In general, it works this way: You withdraw the money from your IRA, close your account, and get a check. You then move the money yourself—by mail, for instance, or on foot—to the new IRA trustee or custodian. *But beware:* You have only 60 days to complete the rollover. Technically, you have to complete the rollover by the 60th day after the day you receive the money.

Watch that Deadline

If you don't make the move in time, the amount you withdrew from your IRA rollover will be treated as ordinary income subject to tax. And you could be faced with a 10 percent early withdrawal penalty to boot.

What's more, the IRS allows only one rollover in every 12-month period. Some IRA owners use rollovers as short-term loans; they pull the cash out, use it to pay a bill, let's say, then replace the money within 60 days. If you have the discipline for this, fine.

Just remember that there are big tax consequences if you don't meet the deadline. To avoid such problems, it's best to stick with direct transfers. They're cleaner, less bothersome, and there are no tax consequences.

The Flexibility of IRAs

The ability to transfer or roll over money from one IRA trustee or custodian to another highlights one of the key benefits IRA investors have: flexibility. It's something you may not get with other retirement savings plans.

A 401(k) or 403(b) plan at work, for example, may let you save conveniently through weekly or monthly payroll deductions. Your employer may also encourage you to save by plopping extra money into your account. But some employer-sponsored plans severely limit your investment options: You may get to choose from among only a handful of mutual funds, for instance, or among only a few funds and your company's stock.

Variable annuities have also become a popular way for investors to save on a tax-deferred basis for long-term goals such as retirement, but these too can be restrictive. The insurance company that offers the annuity might limit your investment choices to only a few so-called subaccounts that offer mutual funds.

The Choice Is Yours

With IRAs, the sky's the limit. You get to pick from among almost any bank, thrift, or credit union or just about any mutual fund company, stock brokerage, or insurer. And having the ability to easily move your money from one IRA custodian or trustee to another is important, not just because of fees, but also because of performance.

Maybe you invested your IRA dollars in a certain high-flying mutual fund only to learn a few years later that the fund's well-regarded manager has jumped ship. Or perhaps you opened an IRA at your friendly neighborhood bank branch, only to find years later—or maybe just months later—that your community bank has been gobbled up by a national giant intent on closing branches and raising fees to meet shareholder demands. It's nice to know you're not locked in; you can move your IRA to another IRA custodian or trustee with relative ease.

Flexibility also is important as you grow older and your investment needs change. If you're nearing retirement, for example, and you expect you'll need to start making withdrawals from your IRA within a fairly short time, you may want to move some, or even all, of your IRA dollars out of an aggressive growth mutual fund or indexed fund and into a comparatively more stable investment, such as a short-term bond fund or money market mutual fund.

If your IRA is in a large brokerage or mutual fund company, moving your IRA money should pose no problem; you can simply transfer the money from one fund to another within the same group or family and take some steps with just a phone call. But if your IRA is in a small fund company, you may not have that option, and you may have to transfer out altogether, which is when the *direct* transfer or rollover option (discussed below) can come in handy.

Switching from Pensions to IRAs

IRAs are also a convenient place to hold money you get from a pension, profit-sharing, or other retirement savings plan at work.

As long as you meet the rules, the transfer or rollover of funds to an IRA from a retirement plan at work will be tax-free, and the money will continue to be sheltered from tax until you withdraw it. But there are some important rules to understand about this step. Before you make a move, you should also consider other options that may leave you better off in the long run.

First, the bad news: If you withdraw money from a retirement plan at work, it may be subject to federal income tax plus a 10 percent early withdrawal penalty if you're under age 59½.

You may sidestep the tax and penalty entirely if you move the money directly into an IRA. The key here, however, is to move it *directly;* if you don't, there's another tax time bomb waiting to explode. If you personally accept a check for money from your retirement plan at work, your employer may hold back 20 percent of it—*even if you later intend to roll it over into an IRA.*

The government figures that if you accept a check for the money in your retirement plan, you're probably going to spend it, or gamble it away, or do anything with it besides putting it into an IRA.

In other words, the government expects that you'll wind up having to pay tax on the amount of money you receive, but the government doesn't want to wait to get its share until you file your annual income tax return. That's why the government requires your employer to hold back 20 percent of the payout.

Avoiding a Penalty

Can you avoid your employer's holding back 20 percent of the IRA payout? You bet. And it's easy. Just tell your employer (or whomever your employer appoints as the plan sponsor or plan administrator) that you want to move the money directly to an IRA. In other words, you want to make a direct transfer. Strangely, the IRS doesn't call this a direct transfer; the IRS uses the term *direct rollover* instead.

Whatever it's called, the bottom line is: Make sure your hands don't touch the money. Arrange things so that the money moves directly to the IRA from your employer's plan. You generally don't have to fret over this because the government requires your employer to give you the option of making a direct transfer (or direct rollover, as the IRS says).

Know your rights.　It's good to know the details of the direct transfer option because some companies still know little about it and thus fail to inform their employees about this valuable option.

It's also possible that your employer won't agree to make the transfer directly to the trustee or custodian of your IRA but instead will only hand over a check directly to you. This can work depending on how the check is written. For instance, if the check is made out to Joe Taxpayer, the company must withhold 20 percent of the amount. But the company generally won't have to withhold the money if the check is made out, for example, to XYZ Co. IRA, for the benefit of Joe Taxpayer, or to ABC Bank, in trust for Joe Taxpayer.

Making a smooth transition.　In other words, your employer can't give you the option of cashing the check yourself; the check *must* be made out to the outfit that's going to be serving as your IRA trustee or custodian.

To ensure that things go smoothly, you might want to contact the outfit you've chosen to hold your IRA—a bank, credit union, insurer, brokerage, or mutual fund company, for example—and let it know what you have planned. The financial institution that's your IRA trustee or custodian may be able to offer some advice and may even let you open the IRA first with the understanding that money will soon be moved into it from your retirement plan at work.

Remember: IRAs that are used for this purpose can only accept money from your pension plan at work that hasn't been taxed yet. You can therefore transfer to an IRA any pretax contributions you made to your pension or retirement plan at work as well as money that your employer contributed to your pension plan account on your behalf plus any earnings that your account has racked up.

But you *cannot* transfer to an IRA any after-tax contributions that you made to your pension or retirement plan at work.

When IRAs Are Not the Best Choice

Keep in mind that moving money into an IRA from a pension or retirement plan at work isn't always the best strategy. In some cases an IRA simply won't work for you or won't work out the best for you.

Here are a few cases where the direct rollover option may not be best:

- Some employers let you keep your money in your pension or retirement plan even after you leave work. If you prefer to take advantage of this opportunity (maybe you like how the money's being invested, or maybe you just don't want to be bothered), that's fine. You generally won't have to start making withdrawals until you reach age 70½, so you can leave the money and let it continue to grow on a tax-deferred basis.

- You'd rather take the money out in a lump sum because you may qualify for favorable tax treatment. (With certain pension plans under certain circumstances, you may treat a lump-sum distribution for federal income tax purposes as if it had come to you over five years instead of one year. If you move your money into an IRA, however, you'll generally lose the option to elect this "forward-averaging" treatment.)
- You want to begin making withdrawals now from your pension plan at work, so you have no need to use an IRA. (Maybe you're at a point where you must begin making minimum annual withdrawals from your pension plan, or maybe you've simply chosen to start taking money out now as part of a series of regular annual withdrawals to help supplement your other income in retirement.)

A Conduit IRA

There may be one other reason you should use an IRA to hold your pension money. Suppose you're changing jobs, or suppose you lose your job but plan to get another one soon. You can move money from the pension plan at your old job directly into an IRA and keep it there until you get a new job.

Your new employer may have a pension plan that accepts money from a pension plan you used to have. If that's the case, you may transfer the money from your IRA to the pension plan at your new job. In this example, you've used the IRA as a kind of temporary parking place or receptacle for your pension money. An IRA that's used for this purpose is known as a "conduit IRA."

The benefits of a conduit IRA are probably obvious. You slip money out of your pension plan at your old job into an IRA and then into a pension plan at your new job, all without any tax consequence.

And while the money was sitting in your IRA, it continued to grow on a tax-deferred basis. That's a neat little trick, but to make it work, you have to keep the conduit IRA free of any other money.

It can't be tainted with additional contributions. It can hold only the money that you contributed from the pension or retirement plan at your old job (along with any money your IRA has earned while serving as a holding tank).

To Sum Up . . .

IRAs offer a key benefit that's often overlooked: flexibility. You can transfer or roll over your money from one IRA custodian or trustee to another. In this respect, IRAs have an edge over some types of pension and retirement savings plans at work, which typically sharply restrict what you can and can't do with your money.

The ability to move your money from one IRA to another also can let you reduce or avoid annual maintenance fees, which have grown in recent years as a way for IRA trustees or custodians to cut their costs.

You may also use an IRA as a conduit, or receptacle, for receiving money from your pension plan at work. This lets your pension money continue to grow without being nicked by taxes, although moving money from a pension to an IRA may not be your best option in a few cases.

For More Information . . .

Fidelity Investments, the Boston-based mutual fund giant, has free kits available that offer details on transferring, or rolling over, money to an IRA from a pension or profit-sharing plan at work.

The kits include the Fidelity *Retirement Planning Guide* and another booklet, *Investing Your Retirement Plan Distribution.*

For a free copy of either or both publications, call 1-800-544-4774, or write: Fidelity Funds, 82 Devonshire St., Boston, MA 02109. If you have access to a computer, contact the company's Web site at www.fidelity.com.

Withdrawing Money from Your IRA

This chapter looks at the tax and other consequences of withdrawing money from a traditional IRA; the 10 percent penalty for withdrawals before you turn 59½ and how to avoid it; steps to take to postpone withdrawals even after you reach 59½ so your account can continue to grow; and the withdrawals required when you turn 70½.

It's probably something you were taught as a child: whenever you enter a building you haven't been in before, look around for the Exit signs because you never know when you'll need them.

The same idea applies to IRAs. It's all well and good to save and save. But what happens when you need to take money out of your IRA to spend it? What are the rules? What will it cost you? And are there any alternatives? In other words, what will happen if you need to get your money and head for the door?

Three Main Exits

If you own an IRA, there are typically three main exits. The one that applies to you generally depends upon your age:

- The government discourages withdrawals from your IRA before you reach age 59½. If you do—that is, make an early withdrawal—you'll generally have to pay federal income tax on it, and you may have to pay a 10 percent federal early withdrawal penalty too.
- If you are between 59½ and 70½ and you withdraw money from your IRA, you'll generally have to pay federal income tax on the money, but you won't be penalized.

- Once you turn 70½, you are *required* to start withdrawing money. Each withdrawal will generally trigger federal income tax, but it won't be penalized—*if* you withdraw enough.

Yes, the rules are a little complicated. And yes, you can't even take money out of your own IRA without getting caught in a tangle of rules and regulations.

Happily, the rules aren't all *that* complicated. And they're a lot easier to understand if you look at them based on age.

Under 59½: Avoiding the Penalty

If you pull money out of your IRA and you haven't reached age 59½, you'll have to note it on your federal income tax return. In effect, you'll say, "I took some money out of my IRA!" and the government will say, "Great! Give us a piece of it! A great big piece!"

The reason you must report your withdrawal is that the money in your account hasn't been taxed yet. You probably claimed a federal income tax deduction for the money you contributed so that, in effect, your contributions were made on a pretax basis. And all the money that your account has earned over the years hasn't been taxed either. It's been growing on a tax-deferred basis year-in, year-out.

It gets worse: When you withdraw money from an IRA before you reach 59½, you'll also face a 10 percent "premature withdrawal" penalty. The penalty is applied to the amount you withdraw, and you must pay the penalty *on top of* any regular income tax you owe. That can be pretty painful.

Suppose you lose your job, for example, and have to withdraw $10,000 from your IRA to help meet expenses. You'll have to report the amount of the withdrawal as income on your tax return, as you know. It'll be treated as ordinary income, the same as wages and salary.

As a result, your $10,000 withdrawal will be subject to tax at your marginal federal tax rate. If you're in the 15 percent bracket in this example, you'll pay $1,500 in federal income tax on your $10,000 withdrawal; in the 28 percent bracket, $2,800; and so on.

A Painful Penalty

In addition to paying tax on your early withdrawal, you'll have to pay a 10 percent penalty. In our example, the penalty would amount to $1,000. You can see how quickly the total tax adds up and how quickly the *net* amount of your withdrawal—the amount you get to keep *after* taxes—can decline. If

Figure 7.1   Avoiding the Penalty

If you take money out of an IRA before you're supposed to, the government may slap you with a 10 percent early withdrawal penalty. You may avoid the penalty if your withdrawal occurs under any of a number of special exceptions:

- You're 59½ or older.
- You're disabled.
- The money is paid out after you die.
- Withdrawal is one in a series of annual withdrawals over your lifetime.
- You're paying for particular medical expenses.
- You're paying for particular health insurance premiums if you've lost your job.
- The money is for first-time homebuyer expenses.
- The money is for college costs.

Source: U.S. Congress, Internal Revenue Service

you're in the 15 percent income tax bracket in our example, you'll have to fork over to the federal government a total of $2,500, which includes $1,500 in income tax and $1,000 in penalty. Out of your total withdrawal of $10,000, you'll be left with only $7,500 after paying tax and penalty.

If you're in the 28 percent bracket in our example, you'll have to hand over $3,800 to the federal government, which includes $2,800 in income tax and $1,000 in penalty. As a result, out of your $10,000 withdrawal, you'll be left with only $6,200 after paying tax and penalty.

In other words, the tax and penalty in this example would gobble up almost 40 percent of the amount you withdrew. And that's not counting any state income tax that may be due. That stings!

In the early 1990s, lots of Americans triggered the penalty. Because of a general trend toward corporate restructuring and downsizing, many people lost their jobs and had to tap their IRAs to help meet expenses as they searched for new jobs or launched their own businesses.

Taxpayers complained about the restrictions; Congress apparently heard their pleas because the government has gradually chipped away at the rules, easing restrictions and providing some relief.

Escaping the Penalty

As a result of Congress easing restrictions, you may now escape the penalty (but not regular income tax) if your withdrawal qualifies as a special exception—even if you haven't reached 59½.

The penalty-free exceptions were once mainly intended for severe hardships only. But Congress has added to the list of special exceptions. There is no penalty now on early withdrawals if they're made under any of the following circumstances (even if you're under 59½):

Disability.   You have to show proof that you can't do any "substantial gainful activity" because of your physical—or mental—condition. And it can't be one of these "I-sprained-my-ankle" deals; a physician must determine that your condition can be expected to result in death or to be of "long, continued and indefinite duration," the IRS says.

Death.   If you die before you turn 59½, the money (or other assets) in your IRA can be pulled out by your beneficiary (or paid to your estate) without penalty.

Part of a series of payments.   This is one exception that's often overlooked and little understood. You can avoid the penalty simply by making a series of withdrawals over a long period of time. But this exception is tricky, and it's easy to trip up because of so many rules.

The withdrawals, for instance, must be part of a series of substantially equal withdrawals made at least once a year. These payments must be made over your life or the joint life expectancy of you and your primary beneficiary. (You may use government life expectancy tables, but there are other ways to calculate these payments; they can be tricky, so be sure to get professional help first.) In other words, you can avoid the penalty if you agree to withdraw money in roughly equal annual installments for the rest of your life. These withdrawals must continue for at least five years or until you reach 59½, whichever turns out to be the *longer* period.

In effect, you may start withdrawing money from your IRA before you turn 59½, without being penalized as long as the withdrawals are part of a regular series of withdrawals (made under an IRS-approved method of calculation). Once you reach 59½, however, you can stop the withdrawals if you want. For example, if you begin making these withdrawals when you're 50, you'll have to continue them until you're 59½, when you can stop. But if you start the withdrawals when you're 57, you'll have to continue them until you're 62, although you can stop then. (Remember the rule: Once you start your series of withdrawals, they must continue for at least five years, or until you turn 59½, whichever is the longer period.)

Medical expenses.   The money you withdraw must be used to pay only for medical expenses to avoid a penalty. These are only expenses for which you haven't been reimbursed (by insurance, for example) and only those expenses that exceed 7.5 percent of your adjusted gross income. In other words, the medical expenses are those you'd normally be able to include on Schedule A of your IRS Form 1040, although technically you don't have to itemize your deductions to qualify for the special exception.

If you have adjusted gross income of $40,000, for example, and you have unreimbursed medical expenses totaling $5,000, you can withdraw $2,000 from your IRA penalty-free to help pay the expenses. Why only $2,000? Because the rules allow penalty-free withdrawals only for expenses that exceed 7.5 percent of your adjusted gross income. In this example, 7.5 percent of your adjusted gross income is $3,000 (.075 times $40,000), so $5,000 minus $3,000 equals $2,000.

Health insurance.   To avoid being penalized, you must be unemployed and use the money you withdraw from your IRA to pay for medical insurance premiums for yourself, your spouse, and/or your dependents. You'll qualify for this exception only if you *meet all four* of these conditions:

1. You lost your job.
2. You received unemployment compensation for 12 consecutive weeks.
3. You make the withdrawal(s) during the year you received the unemployment benefits *or* the following year.
4. You make the withdrawals no later than 60 days after you've gotten another job.

College expenses.   You must use the money for so-called qualified higher education expenses either for yourself, your spouse, or any child or grandchild of yours or your spouse, according to IRS rules. (You don't have to claim the child or grandchild as a dependent on your tax return.) The expenses include tuition at a postsecondary educational institution, the IRS says, as well as any fees, supplies, books, and equipment required for enrollment or attendance at any eligible educational institution (such as a college, university, vocational school, or other postsecondary institution that's eligible to take part in student aid programs run by the U.S. Department of Education). The expenses also include room and board if the student is enrolled at least half-time. And the expenses can be for undergraduate *and* graduate study. Before you make any withdrawal, however, you'll first have to reduce the amount of education expenses by certain amounts you've already received, such as Pell grants, tax-free scholarships, or tax-free educational assistance provided by an employer.

First-time homebuyer costs. To qualify for this penalty-free exception, you must use the money to buy, build, or rebuild a house that'll serve as the "principal residence" for you, your spouse, or any child, grandchild, or "ancestor" (such as a parent or grandparent) of yours or your spouse. The money may also be used to pay for any "usual or reasonable" settlement, financing, or other such closing costs, according to the government's rules. There's a 120-day deadline for using the money, which can't exceed $10,000 over your lifetime, and the clock generally starts ticking at the point of withdrawal.

The government is pretty loose in defining who exactly qualifies as a "first-time homebuyer." In general, you don't have to be buying a house for the first time in your life. The IRS will consider you a first-time homebuyer as long as you—or your spouse if you're married—haven't had an ownership interest in a principal residence during the two years before you acquire your next principal residence. Suppose you owned your own house, sold it in 1996, then moved into a condominium as a temporary rental. In 1999 you yank $10,000 out of your IRA to buy a house. You won't have to pay the 10 percent penalty on the $10,000 withdrawal because at least two years have passed since you sold your old house. (You'll still have to report the amount of the withdrawal—$10,000 in this example—as income on your tax return, but you won't also be penalized even though you're under 59½.)

Other Penalty-Free Moves

Some actions you can take, in addition to fitting the circumstances described above, automatically avoid the 10 percent penalty. Here's a quick summary of some other actions you can take or conditions in which the 10 percent penalty is sidestepped:

- You transfer directly money or other assets from one IRA to another or from certain types of pension plans to an IRA.
- You roll over money or other assets from one IRA to another within the 60-day limit.
- Contributions of after-tax dollars to an IRA are known as "nondeductible" contributions, and they avoid a penalty if you withdraw them. If you withdraw any money from your account that your nondeductible contributions earned over the years, however, the *earnings* will be subject to the penalty—if you're under 59½ and don't meet any of the main exceptions. (For more on nondeductible IRAs, see Chapter 10.)
- Transfers made under a divorce decree or separate maintenance decree are generally considered tax-free and penalty-free (whether the name on an IRA is changed or assets from one spouse's IRA are transferred to the former spouse's IRA).

- "Timely withdrawals" of money you contribute to an IRA avoid the 10 percent penalty. Say you contribute $2,000 to your traditional IRA for a given year but claim no deduction for it, and you withdraw the $2,000—as well as any earnings it generated—before the due date of your tax return for that year. In this case, the $2,000 you withdraw won't be subject to either tax or penalty. (But any earnings that your $2,000 contribution generated will be taxed and generally will be subject to the 10 percent early withdrawal penalty if you haven't turned 59½.)

Between 59½ and 70½: The Tax Consequences

You've been stashing away money for your retirement, resisting time and again the temptation to spend. Perhaps now is the time you've chosen to enjoy the money you've saved. No more scrimping, no more sacrifices. Now is the time you decide to start withdrawing money.

Can you do it? Yes. Of course, it would be better if you could leave the money in your account as long as possible so it could continue to grow sheltered from taxes. But if you really need to withdraw money between 59½ and 70½, it's nice to know you can get it if you want it.

But how do you go about it? Do you just take what you need and skip the details? If only it were so easy. The problem, as ever, is taxes, because whenever you withdraw money from a traditional IRA, you'll generally be taxed.

Things could be worse—some retirees have no IRA from which to withdraw money. To cover their needs in retirement, they rely solely on Social Security and maybe a pension—if they're lucky.

You, on the other hand, have savings, even though whatever you withdraw from your traditional IRA is potentially subject to being taxed. The remainder, however, can keep growing sheltered from taxation, at least for the time being.

Some Tax Planning

Before you plunge ahead and start pulling your money out of your IRA, take a few minutes to think about the consequences. Some careful planning now can save you money in the future. Already there are some points in your favor. For instance:

- You won't be penalized. Remember that if you withdraw money from an IRA before you reach age 59½, the withdrawal generally is subject to a 10 percent penalty. But if you withdraw money *after* you turn 59½, you won't be subject to this penalty at all. Congratulations!

- You don't have to worry about the "success tax" anymore. What does that mean? Incredible as it may seem, there was a time—and it wasn't long ago—that you faced a 15 percent so-called excess accumulations tax on withdrawals from your IRA, even in retirement. The law stated, in general, that if you withdrew a total of more than $155,000 from your IRAs, pension plans, and tax-sheltered annuities in any given year, you'd be punished with a 15 percent tax on the amount above $155,000. For working hard all your life, for saving a lot—for doing all the things you were supposed to do—you'd be slammed by yet another tax. A 1996 tax law temporarily suspended this penalty, and with the Taxpayer Relief Act of 1997, the government scrapped the success tax altogether.

Withdrawals as Income

What tax complications then *do* you face?

Any withdrawal you make will have to be included in your gross income for the year in which you make it. In other words, any withdrawal is going to be subject to federal income tax. If the withdrawal is large enough, it could wind up increasing your taxable income and bump you into a higher tax bracket.

Furthermore, a withdrawal from an IRA could boost your so-called provisional income, making some part of your Social Security benefits subject to taxation. (If some of your benefits are already taxed, an IRA withdrawal could mean a greater share of your Social Security benefits would be taxed.)

Losing the Benefits of Compounding

In addition to possibly boosting your provisional income, any money you withdraw from an IRA—even in retirement—won't have the chance to keep growing inside your account sheltered from tax. So you lose the chance for more tax-deferred growth, not to mention the magic of compound interest.

Experts usually suggest that you delay as long as possible making any withdrawals from your IRA. But what can you do instead if you really need some money? The answer: consider any other savings or investments you may have. Think about withdrawing the money that'll have the least tax consequences.

Make the Most of Your Withdrawal

Suppose you need $1,000 to pay for a trip, to buy someone a gift, or to just go on a splurge, and you've got a few options. Below are a few ways to get the money with the least tax complications:

- Withdraw first from a bank savings account or another taxable account, such as a bank money market account or a money market mutual fund. You've put after-tax dollars into these accounts, and the earnings have probably already been taxed, so you won't be taxed again when you make your withdrawal. What's more, of all your investments these accounts may be generating the lowest yield, so think about tapping them first (as long as you'll still have some money left over to cover emergencies).
- Consider cashing in shares of a mutual fund or selling some shares of stock. True, this step has tax consequences too, but they're not as bad as they once were. Remember: The top federal tax rate on capital gains from the profit on the sale of stock, mutual funds, and similar assets used to be 28 percent. The government, however, changed the rules and now, for assets held at least 18 months, the most you'll pay in federal capital gains tax is 20 percent (if you're normally in the 28 percent federal bracket or higher) or 10 percent (if you're normally in the 15 percent bracket.) And starting January 1, 2001, the maximum capital gains tax rates move even lower: For assets held longer than five years, you'll generally pay a maximum federal tax of 18 percent (if you're normally in the 28 percent bracket or higher) or 8 percent (if you're normally in the 15 percent bracket).
- If you have more than one traditional IRA and you need to tap at least one of them, think about withdrawing from the one that's earning the least. For example, if one of your IRAs is in a bank account paying 5 percent annual interest and another is in a corporate bond mutual fund that's been generating an 8 percent annual return, tap the 5 percent account first and let your 8 percent IRA continue to grow.

Over 70½: When You Must Withdraw

There'll come a time when you must start withdrawing money from your traditional IRAs even if you don't want to.

Maybe you've got enough money coming in from Social Security, pensions, and savings to cover all your expenses and then some. Or maybe you just live frugally out of habit or as a matter of principle, so you'd like to postpone withdrawing money from your traditional IRA a few more years. But you can't.

The government says you can't keep money in an IRA indefinitely. These are, after all, individual *retirement* accounts. They're supposed to supply you with income during your retirement; the government didn't set them up as a tool for passing wealth along to the next generation.

The government gave you a tax break for contributing to your IRA and another break by letting you defer, or postpone, tax on the earnings inside your account. When you retire, however, the government wants to get at least a piece of the action before you die, so tax law requires—that is, mandates— that you make withdrawals at a specified point.

A Strict Rule

The government takes mandatory withdrawals seriously. If you don't make the required withdrawal at the required time—or if you withdraw some money but not enough—you'll face a penalty. And it's a mean, punishing penalty.

In general, if you don't withdraw money from a regular IRA when you're supposed to, the IRS whacks you with a 50 percent penalty. That's right: 50 percent! The penalty is figured on the amount you should have withdrawn. Here's how it works: Suppose you were required to withdraw $1,000 in a given year, but you didn't. You refused. Or maybe you just forgot (despite all the notices your IRA custodian or trustee mailed you). In this example, the IRS would require you to pay an excise tax of $500. Ouch!

You can get around the penalty only in highly unusual circumstances. Consider: In 1991 Rhode Island was plunged into a banking crisis. A total of 45 banks and credit unions were ordered closed by then-Governor Bruce G. Sundlun after their private insurer of deposits collapsed. Federal regulators later declared that Sundlun had made the right decision. In fact, they said, it was the only prudent choice at the time, given the circumstances.

But among all the depositors whose accounts were frozen, some were IRA holders and some of them were nearing the deadline for making required withdrawals. They wanted to withdraw money, if only to avoid the dreaded 50 percent excise tax. But they couldn't make the mandatory withdrawals because their accounts were frozen. Still, the IRS wouldn't budge: If these depositors didn't make the required withdrawals, they'd be penalized, the IRS said.

The government eventually had to institute a special measure to relieve the depositors of their obligation to make the required withdrawals until their accounts were released.

The bottom line? If you're facing the deadline, make the withdrawal according to the rules so you can avoid the painful penalty; don't expect the government to bail you out.

A Tangled Web

How do you go about figuring how much you must withdraw? Unfortunately, it's complicated. In fact, it's an absolute swamp of tangled rules and regulations, and it's very easy to trip up.

Some IRA trustees or custodians may do the work for you for a small fee or no fee as a service to their customers. Typically, this work is done by the "operations people" at a bank, brokerage, or mutual fund company, for example. These are the behind-the-scenes workers who generally know the rules, the exceptions, and everything in between, so you can rely on them in the main.

If the service isn't available—or even if it is, but you want to double-check their work—you may want to consult an accountant or someone else who's familiar with exactly how these thorny rules apply to you.

To Sum Up . . .

If you withdraw money from a regular IRA before you turn 59½, the amount of each withdrawal will generally be taxed and penalized. There are some exceptions to the penalty but not to the tax. Once you reach 59½, you can withdraw money without penalty—but it will still be subject to tax. And once you reach 70½, you absolutely have to start making withdrawals from your traditional IRA(s) even if you don't want to.

For More Information . . .

Calculating your minimum required withdrawals from a regular IRA generally isn't a do-it-yourself deal because it can be so complicated. But if you plan to do the work yourself or you just want to have an idea of how it's done, see the following chapter, which is devoted entirely to this topic and includes tips on where to go for more information.

Figuring Your Minimum Withdrawals

Chapter 8 explains how to calculate the minimum withdrawals you must make from a regular IRA after you turn 70½; how to figure your life expectancy; how beneficiaries play a role; and your options.

It's the rule that a lot of taxpayers dread: when you turn 70½, the government requires you to start taking at least a minimum amount out of your IRA account(s).

Why is that so bad? Some people simply don't want to take money out of their regular IRAs—ever. They have enough money to get by so they really don't need to tap their IRA. And they know that each withdrawal counts as income for tax purposes, so every dollar they withdraw is going to be taxed.

If that weren't bad enough, figuring the amount of each withdrawal is a real pain. It's challenging. It's complicated. There are tons of rules and a lot of ways to run afoul of those rules, which is why many IRA holders leave the job to a professional. But you *can* do it yourself. The following sections should help.

A Summary of the Rules

The IRS gives you a choice: withdraw the entire balance from your account or start making periodic withdrawals by a certain point.

Most people choose to make periodic withdrawals mainly because of the tax consequences. A lump sum withdrawal could bump you into a higher tax bracket, at least for one year, and could subject part of your Social Security benefits to taxation.

Taxation is not the only reason people usually choose periodic withdrawals. By withdrawing only some of your IRA dollars each year, you let the rest of your account continue to grow on a tax-deferred basis.

The First Withdrawal

If you decide to make a series of withdrawals instead of the lump sum option, you must make your first minimum withdrawal—what the IRS calls your first "required minimum distribution"—in the year you turn 70½. (The IRS calls this your "required beginning date.")

You don't really have to make the withdrawal that year; you can wait until April 1 of the following year. In fact, whenever you ask a tax professional what the deadline is, the response is almost invariably the same: You have until April 1 of the year *following* the year in which you reach age 70½.

Keep in mind that waiting until the last moment can cause some complications (which we'll look at in a moment).

Periodic Withdrawals

If you choose to make periodic withdrawals, you generally must make them based on a schedule that takes into account your life expectancy or the joint life expectancies of you and your beneficiary. "Life expectancy" generally means how long you're expected to live. "Joint life expectancy" takes into account how long you and your IRA's beneficiary, such as your spouse, are going to live. The life expectancy figures are listed in tables that are published by the government, and they're easy to get. (More on that later.)

How do you know when the withdrawal deadline is near? It sounds more complicated than it really is. All you really have to do is keep track of your age.

When the Time Is Right

If you were born in September 1929, for example, you'll be 70½ in March 2000. You generally therefore must make your first withdrawal by December 31, 2000. Because the government is willing to cut you a little slack, it gives you the option to extend the deadline for your first minimum required withdrawal by about three months, pushing the deadline off into the following year.

In our example then, you'd technically have until April 1, 2001, to make your first minimum required withdrawal from your IRA. (Remember the rule: Withdraw by April 1 of the year *following* the year in which you reach age 70½.)

"Bunching" Causes Problems

Should you wait until the last minute? Not necessarily. The trouble is that you could wind up making two of the required minimum withdrawals in a single tax year, which could increase your income sharply for that year. And that could bump you into a higher tax bracket, as discussed earlier and explained below.

Consider our example. You could make your required minimum withdrawal in the year 2000. But suppose you decide to wait until March 2001 to do it? Fine. You've met the deadline. The trouble is that the next scheduled withdrawal in this example must be made by December 31, 2001.

The problem is that although you make the withdrawal by April 1, 2001, the government counts it as having been made for the year 2000—but only for purposes of setting a starting point for what will be your first in a series of annual required minimum withdrawals. And for these purposes only, the withdrawal you make by December 31, 2001, is counted as having been done for the year 2001.

So far, so good. *But for income tax purposes, both withdrawals in this example will be counted as having been made in 2001.* As a result, the amount of both withdrawals will be added to your income for 2001.

When Two Withdrawals Are Better than One

Two withdrawals in one tax year may not be a bad idea for some people in certain circumstances. Maybe you've decided to postpone that first withdrawal until April 1, 2001, because you expect your income to decline in 2001; maybe you've got a part-time job right now, but the job will end in 2000. Therefore, making two withdrawals in the same tax year won't be so bad because your income will be lower for that year anyway. For other taxpayers, on the other hand, bunching two withdrawals from an IRA in the same tax year can cause tax problems, as described above.

How can you get around bunching two withdrawals? In this example, you may simply make your first required minimum withdrawal in the year 2000 (you have that option). Then you may take your next required minimum withdrawal in 2001. In this way, you've met the rules, but you've also spaced out your withdrawals, one per tax year. This lets you avoid getting two helpings of extra income into just one tax year—a neat little bit of tax planning that can save you money.

Just keep in mind that your later minimum withdrawals must be made once a year by the end of each calendar year. Remember, too, that you don't have to withdraw the money in a single lump sum each year; you can always make the withdrawals in installments—monthly or quarterly, for example—as long as they all add up by the end of the year to the minimum amount required to be withdrawn for that year. And if you change your mind later, you can always withdraw *more* than the minimum required amount. You're not locked into the schedule, though, of course, you can never withdraw *less* than the minimum required amount.

How Much You Must Withdraw

Now that you know *when* to make your minimum required withdrawals, how do you know *how much* to withdraw?

The IRS has a special booklet, Publication 590, that includes the worksheets you'll need to figure out how much to withdraw. And remember that your IRA trustee or custodian may be willing to help, or even do the work for you, for a small fee or no fee. (Don't be afraid to ask your trustee if this service is available.)

Still, it may be helpful—though painful—to see for yourself how to calculate how much you must withdraw, if only to make sure that your IRA trustee or your accountant has done it right. It's not that hard, but it takes a little time and a little concentration. These four steps summarize how to do the calculation:

1. You first need to know your account balance, so check your account statement for December 31 of the year *before* the year for which your withdrawal will count. Suppose you've decided to make a withdrawal for the year 2000. In this example, you'll need to know your account balance as of December 31, 1999. (If you reach age 70½ in the year 2000, you can wait until early in 2001 to make your first minimum required withdrawal. But even if you do wait until the last minute to make the withdrawal, it still counts for the year 2000 in this example, so your account balance as of December 31, 1999, is still the one to use.) For future years, remember to use the account balance at the end of the previous year. For example, to help figure out the amount you must withdraw for the year 2002, use your account balance as of December 31, 2001.

2. Now check the government's life expectancy tables, keeping in mind that these tables are only government estimates and are not updated all the time. Nevertheless, these are the figures you have to use. You'll find the tables in a current copy of IRS Publication 590. You can also find more elaborate life expectancy tables in IRS Publication 939. Both publications are free. (To order, see "For More Information . . ." at the end of this chapter.)

3. The life expectancy tables will give you a key figure, known as the "divisor" or "multiple." (For convenience, we'll just call this figure your life expectancy "factor.")

4. The last step is simple: Divide your account balance by your life expectancy factor. The result is the minimum amount that you must withdraw from your IRA.

Figure 8.1   Figuring Your Life Expectancy

A 71-year-old man, whose beneficiary is his 56-year-old wife, may use the "Joint Life and Last Survivor Expectancy" table to help figure the amount of his minimum required withdrawal from his IRA. To do this, he reads down the first column to find his age, then reads across the top to find his wife's age. The point where they intersect is the "divisor" (or life expectancy factor). He then divides his $29,000 IRA balance by the divisor (29). This means his first required withdrawal must be at least $1,000.

Ages	55	56	57	58
68	30.2	29.5	28.8	28.1
69	30.1	29.3	28.6	27.8
70	29.9	29.1	28.4	27.6
71	29.7	29.0	28.2	27.5
72	29.6	28.8	28.1	27.3

Note: This is excerpted from the full table that appears in Appendix B.
Source: Internal Revenue Service

Putting It All Together

Here's an example of how these pieces fit together. Suppose you must make your first minimum withdrawal in 2000, and the balance in your IRA as of December 31, 1999, is $100,000. Let's also say that you've looked through the tables and you've come upon the factor of 20. Now, divide $100,000 by 20. The answer is $5,000. That's how much you must withdraw, at a minimum, by April 1, 2001, to meet the rules and avoid the penalty.

Of course, as mentioned earlier, you might be better off withdrawing the $5,000 in the year 2000 in this example instead of waiting until April 1, 2001, to avoid having two withdrawals bunched into the same tax year.

Waiting 'til the Last Moment

But what if you *do* wait until the last minute to make your first required minimum withdrawal? How do you figure out the amount of your next required minimum withdrawal? It's a little complicated, but here's an example that may help:

Suppose you turned 70½ in early 1998 and your wife turned 56 in the same year. Your account balance was $29,000 at the end of the previous year (1997).

If you check the joint life expectancy table in Figure 8.1, you'll come up with a factor of 29.

It's pretty easy to figure out your first minimum required withdrawal: just divide your account balance as of December 31, 1997 ($29,000), by the factor you found in Figure 8.1. The answer is $1,000, which is how much you must withdraw.

Let's also say that in this example you wait to make that first withdrawal until April 1, 1999. In other words, you decide to take advantage of the three extra months the government gives you to make your first required withdrawal, so you delay making the withdrawal until early 1999.

How do you figure your next withdrawal, the amount you're required to withdraw by December 31, 1999? You use your account balance as of December 31, 1998, *but* you first subtract the amount of your first required withdrawal ($1,000).

Yes, that's right: even though you didn't actually withdraw the $1,000 until early 1999, you must still subtract it from your December 31, 1998, balance. (This special rule applies *only* for figuring the amount of your minimum withdrawal for your *second* required withdrawal.)

Say that your IRA earned enough in 1998 to grow to about $30,450 by the end of that year. But for purposes of calculating your second required withdrawal in this example, you must subtract the $1,000 that you withdrew for 1998 (even though you actually withdrew it in early 1999). The number therefore that you must use to calculate your second required withdrawal—the one that'll count for 1999—is $29,450 (which is your actual December 31, 1998, balance of $30,450 minus your first required withdrawal of $1,000).

What factor will you use? Well, that depends on what method you choose. But more on that later. For now, let's just say you use a method that will reduce your factor by one each year. Back to our example: to figure out the amount of your second required withdrawal, just divide the revised account balance of $29,450 by a factor of 28. The answer is about $1,050, which is how much you must withdraw by December 31, 1999.

If you understand all that clearly, you should congratulate yourself and take a moment to catch your breath because things only get more complicated from here.

Working with the Tables

Let's start with the life expectancy tables. Which one you use generally depends on which one applies to your circumstances. For instance, if you own an IRA and have no beneficiary, you'll use the "Single Life Expectancy" table, which is easy to use. An excerpt is shown in Figure 8.2. You just find your age in the column that's labeled "Age." To locate your life expectancy

Figure 8.2   Single Life Expectancy

To figure the amount of each periodic IRA withdrawal over your life only, use the "Single Life Expectancy" table. If you're 71, for example, simply read down the first column to find your age. The number next to your age, the "divisor," is 15.3. So divide your IRA balance by 15.3 to find out how much you must withdraw.

Age	Divisor
68	17.6
69	16.8
70	16.0
71	15.3
72	14.6
73	13.9
74	13.2
75	12.5
76	11.9

Note: This is excerpted from a full table that appears in Appendix B.
Source: Internal Revenue Service

factor, read across into the next column, which is labeled "Divisor." If you're age 71, for example, your life expectancy factor will be 15.3. By dividing your account balance by that number, you'll see how much you have to withdraw.

What if you have a beneficiary? You may use the table that's officially labeled "Joint Life and Last Survivor Expectancy." Excerpts from this table are shown in Figure 8.3. By using this table, you generally may make lower minimum withdrawals than if you used the "Single Life Expectancy" table because you're taking into account the lives of two people, not just one. And it is hoped your beneficiary is younger than you are!

The numbers in the far left column of the table, reading down, correspond to *your age*. The numbers across the top of the other columns generally correspond to the *age of your beneficiary*.

Find the point where these two figures meet, which is your life expectancy factor. And that's the number you use to help you find out how much you should withdraw, at a minimum, from your IRA. (The tables also generally work in reverse: You may find your age in the numbers across the top of the table and your beneficiary's age along the left side reading down.)

Figure 8.3   Using the Joint Life Expectancy Table

If you're 72, your beneficiary is 68, and you're using the "Joint Life and Last Survivor Expectancy Table," find your age by running your finger down the first column. Find your beneficiary's age by running your finger across the top column. Now find the point in the body of the table where these two figures meet. The divisor is 20.8. Divide your IRA balance by 20.8 to find out how much money you must withdraw.

Ages	67	68	69	70
70	22.0	21.5	21.1	20.6
71	21.7	21.2	20.7	20.2
72	21.3	20.8	20.3	19.8
73	21.0	20.5	20.0	19.4
74	20.8	20.2	19.6	19.1

Note: This is an excerpt from the full table that appears in Appendix B. Note that in the full table you may also find your age by reading across the top and your beneficiary's age by reading down the first column. The result will be the same as above.
Source: Internal Revenue Service

How the Joint Life Expectancy Table Works

Still confused? I don't blame you. It's not easy. But you won't find it so hard once you try it. Figure 8.3 shows part of a joint life expectancy table from the 1997 edition of IRS Publication 590. (For current tables, check the most recent IRS publications.) How does it work? Suppose you're 72 and your beneficiary is 68. To find your age, look at the first column on the far left of the table and read down. (You might find it helpful to circle the number with a pencil.) To find your beneficiary's age, look at the very top line of the table and read across, to the right. (You might want to circle that number too.) Now find the exact spot in the body of the table where the two points intersect. The answer is 20.8, which is your life expectancy factor.

Your next step is to divide your account balance by your life expectancy factor to figure out how much you should withdraw. For example, if your account balance is $50,000, you must withdraw a minimum of about $2,404 for the year (because $50,000 divided by 20.8 equals $2,403.85).

Choosing a Method

Once you've figured out your first minimum withdrawal, it can be fairly easy to figure out the amount of each minimum withdrawal for later years. Once you've found your life expectancy factor for that first minimum required withdrawal, you can use the same factor to figure out all future withdrawals. Just subtract one for each year that passes. The experts call this the "declining years" method, or simply the "minus one" method.

Using the "Minus One" Method

How does it work? Here's an example. If the factor for the first year's minimum required withdrawal is 20.8, you'd use a factor of 19.8 for the second year, 18.8 for the third year, and so on. As each year goes by, you simply divide your account balance as of the previous December 31 by your life expectancy factor, reduced by one from the year before.

That sounds easy. And it is. But there is another way to do it. You can refigure your life expectancy each year, instead of just subtracting by one. In other words, for each year you make a withdrawal, you may perform the same calculation you did for your very first minimum required withdrawal. The experts call this the "recalculation" method.

Saving Money by Refiguring Withdrawals

Yes, it takes extra time and more effort. So why would anyone do it? Because recalculating your life expectancy each year can result in a somewhat lower minimum withdrawal than you'd otherwise have to make.

How can this be? If you don't recalculate, remember that you reduce the factor by one each year in effect. This generally means that for each year you're alive, you're expected to live one less year.

That's not how it necessarily works in real life, however. Suppose, for instance, that you're 70 this year. According to the "Single Life Expectancy" table, the government estimates that you're going to live another 16 years.

The next year, you're 71. Does that mean you have only 15 years left? It does if you use the minus one method because you must reduce your life expectancy by one each year. But look again at the government's tables. If you're 71, the government expects you to live another 15.3 years, not just 15 years. Why? In general, the longer you live, the longer you're expected to live.

In other words, the government is saying, "Not dead yet? Good for you! By making it this far, you've beaten our original estimates. Maybe it's because of good genes or good clean living, so we're giving you some extra points!"

Extra points mean extra money.   It's really no laughing matter because these extra points mean extra money in your pocket. How? Remember that the higher the factor, the lower the amount your annual withdrawal will have to be. The smaller the annual withdrawal, the less income you'll have to report to the government on your income tax return for the year.

This generally means you'll have to pay less tax. And meanwhile, the money that stays in your account continues to grow on a tax-deferred basis, so in our example, it's better to have a factor of 15.3 than a factor of 15. That's what recalculation is all about.

With the minus one method, you must reduce your factor each year by one. But by recalculating each year, you use your true age and go back and check the life expectancy tables every year. In this way, you may wind up being able to reduce your factor by less than one.

A Few Pointers

There are still a few quick points to keep in mind:

- You generally have to choose recalculation *before* you make your first minimum required withdrawal. In general then, you must make this choice by April 1 of the year following the year in which you reach age 70½. And once you choose, that's it: you're locked in. It's an *irrevocable* decision.
- Although the law lets you choose whether to recalculate your life expectancy each year (or the joint life expectancy of yourself and your beneficiary), your IRA trustee or custodian may not allow it. Your account documents will show whether your plan gives you the choice. (And if you're not old enough yet to have to worry about this choice, it's a good point to keep in mind when deciding where to open an IRA.)
- If you want to refigure your own life expectancy each year, just use your age as of your birthday during that year.
- If your spouse is your beneficiary, and you want to refigure the life expectancies of yourself and your spouse beneficiary each year, use your ages as of your birthdays during the year.
- If your main beneficiary is *not* your spouse, you may recalculate only *your* life expectancy but *not* your beneficiary's (and this procedure is pretty tricky, so make sure you get some professional help with it).

For more details about death, taxes, and IRAs, see the next chapter.

Okay so far? Fine. Unfortunately, it gets more complicated—a lot more complicated—and this is one reason you may want to have a professional do the job for you.

A Third Table

There are two basic life expectancy tables, but in certain circumstances you may have to use a third. Here's a quick review of each of the three:

- If your IRA doesn't have a beneficiary (or if your IRA's beneficiary is your estate or another entity that isn't a person), you use the "Single Life Expectancy" table.
- If you have a beneficiary, you may use the "Joint Life and Last Survivor Expectancy" table instead of the single life table. (The joint table takes into account the life expectancy, in years, of both you and your beneficiary.)
- If you have more than one beneficiary for your account, you may still use the joint life expectancy table. But you must base your calculations on your age and on the age of the *oldest* primary beneficiary.
- If your primary beneficiary is not your spouse, you may still use the joint life expectancy table referred to above. But what if that beneficiary is more than ten years younger than you are? A special rule kicks in. It's known as the "minimum distribution incidental benefit" rule. Here's what it means: in effect, you have to pretend that the beneficiary is precisely ten years younger than you are even if the beneficiary is really a lot younger. Here's how it works: you check the joint life expectancy table, as you normally would, using your and your beneficiary's actual age. Then you must also check another table, called the "Minimum Distribution Incidental Benefit" table. Each table will give you a factor, but you must use the factor that's the *smaller* of the two.

Pretending

Why would you have to pretend that your beneficiary is ten years younger than you are?

As you know, the government wants to make sure that your IRA is used mainly to give you retirement benefits during your lifetime. As a result, the government has rules that are set up in such a way that your IRA will have only "incidental" benefits left in it for your beneficiary after you die. (That's why it's called the minimum distribution incidental benefit rule!)

How does it work? If you named a child as your main beneficiary, for example, and used the normal joint life expectancy table, you'd come up with an unusually high factor, which would sharply reduce the minimum amount you'd have to withdraw. And the lower the amount you withdraw, the less you have to report as income, and the less tax you have to pay.

A lower factor means larger withdrawals. The government doesn't want you to pay less tax. It wants you to come up with a low factor so you'll be

Figure 8.4   Minimum Distribution Table

If your IRA beneficiary is not your spouse and the beneficiary is more than ten years younger than you, you'll have to take a few steps to help figure the amount of your minimum required withdrawal, including use of the "Table for Determining Applicable Divisor for MDIB." This table, excerpted below, is easy to use. Just find your age and use the "applicable divisor" next to your age. If you're 71, the answer is 25.3.

Age	Divisor
70	26.2
71	25.3
72	24.4
73	23.5
74	22.7
75	21.8
76	20.9
77	20.1

Note: This is an excerpt from the full table that appears in Appendix B.
Source: Internal Revenue Service

required to withdraw a larger amount. This means more income you have to report on your tax return and a higher tax bill.

Suppose your IRA balance is $100,000. You're 71 and your daughter, who's the primary beneficiary of your IRA, is 41. If you could get away with using your daughter's actual age, you'd check the joint life expectancy table and come up with a factor of 41.9. To figure the minimum withdrawal, you'd divide $100,000 by 41.9 and you'd have to withdraw only about $2,400.

That'd be great—*if* you could do it. But you can't. You have to use the minimum distribution rule. In other words, you have to pretend that your beneficiary is only ten years younger than you are.

Using the MDIB Table

The minimum distribution incidental benefit (MDIB) table takes into account that your beneficiary is considered only ten years younger than you. It does the pretending for you.

To see how it works in our example, look up your age only on the MDIB table, as shown in Figure 8.4. The factor you must use is right next to your age, and in our example the factor is 25.3.

So now you have two factors: 41.9 (from the joint life expectancy table, using your and your beneficiary daughter's actual age), and 25.3 (from the minimum distribution incidental benefit table, using just your actual age). Which do you use? The smaller number (of course!). As a result, you now must divide your $100,000 account balance by 25.3, which means your minimum withdrawal is roughly $4,000.

In other words, by requiring you to use another, stricter formula, the government makes you withdraw about $1,600 *more* than you would have to if you were able to use your daughter's true age in this example. And that's $1,600 *more* in income that you'll have to report on your tax return for the year. If you're in the 28 percent income tax bracket, you'll wind up paying about $500 *more* in federal income tax.

Helpful Hints

Not only is this stuff complicated, it's also really tricky. Here are a few other points to keep in mind:

- What if you want to change your beneficiary? You can do it at any time. If you pick a new beneficiary before you've started making your minimum annual withdrawals, you can just follow the steps listed earlier to figure out the amount of your withdrawals. But if you change your beneficiary *after* you've started making your minimum annual withdrawals, there's a rule you must follow: If the new beneficiary has a shorter life expectancy than the beneficiary you dropped, you have to refigure the period over which you make future withdrawals—and use in your calculations the new beneficiary (the one with the shorter life expectancy). But if the new beneficiary has a longer life expectancy than the beneficiary you dropped, you generally cannot refigure; you've got to continue with the same formula you used with the beneficiary you dropped (because the beneficiary you dropped has a shorter life expectancy).
- What if you have more than one beneficiary listed on your account? In other words, what if you have a number of beneficiaries on one IRA and all of them are different people? How do you go about figuring life expectancy? You have to use the oldest beneficiary. In other words, you must use the beneficiary who has the shortest life expectancy. You can see the impact: the older the beneficiary, the shorter the life expectancy. The shorter the life expectancy, the smaller the factor you'll get from the tables. The smaller the factor, the bigger your withdrawal. The bigger your withdrawal, the more tax you'll have to pay!
- What if you have more than one IRA? The bad news is that you must do a calculation for *each* of your IRAs. Why? The government says you

have to figure out the minimum amount of money that must be with-drawn from each account. And the minimum may be different for each of your IRAs, depending on the balance in each account and the pri-mary beneficiary you've named for each account. But here again the trustee or custodian for each of your IRAs may be willing to help you do the calculations and may even do it themselves for a small fee or no fee. Nevertheless, the whole process can mean more paperwork, more time, and more effort for you. The good news is that if you have more than one IRA, you don't actually have to make a minimum withdrawal from each of them (even if your IRAs are held in different places—a bank and a mutual fund, for example—and even though your trustees or custodians may be bombarding you with notices about required withdrawals.) To meet the rules, you can simply add up all the amounts that you're required to withdraw from each of your IRAs, then with-draw the money from just one account. (You may have to let all your IRA trustees or custodians know exactly what you're planning to do.)

- If you have more than one IRA, and you've figured the minimum required withdrawal for each, but you now want to make just one big withdrawal to cover the requirement, from which account should you make the withdrawal? Here again, let common sense be your guide. If one account is earning less than the others, and its future prospects don't look especially good, that's a good place from which to start mak-ing your withdrawals.

- A lot of attention gets paid to delaying your IRA withdrawals as long as possible and then withdrawing the absolute minimum amount. But if you need to withdraw money *before* you reach 70½, it's okay. Just remember that you must pay federal income tax on the amount you withdraw.

- If you withdraw money from an IRA as an annuity that you bought from an insurance company, special rules apply. Contact your insur-ance company for details.

- If you made nondeductible contributions to your traditional IRA (as dis-cussed in Chapter 10) as well as deductible contributions, a portion of your withdrawals won't be taxed at all; because your nondeductible con-tributions were made with after-tax dollars, they can't be taxed again.

To Sum Up . . .

There are lots of details and lots of formulas, so it's tempting to be over-whelmed by it all. But a flip side to all of this is that you have lots of options. And that's an important point to remember when it comes to withdrawing money from your IRA.

If you're in the pleasant position of not having to take money from your traditional IRA until the last moment, when you're absolutely required to, you have a lot of choices to make. Yes, that's complicated, but it also means you have lots of opportunities too.

Before you make a move, your best bet is to seek professional guidance. Remember: A lot of the rules for required minimum withdrawals aren't easily available. Some are in the form of regulations that have been proposed—but not finalized—for more than ten years! The IRS is still working on them.

An accountant, tax lawyer, or similar professional will have ready access to these regulations and should be able to figure out how best to apply them to your personal circumstances, after taking into account your overall financial picture, income needs, and estate plans. You can go it alone in this area, but you put yourself—and your beneficiaries—at risk.

For More Information . . .

This chapter offers only a brief overview of the general rules that govern minimum required withdrawals, and keep in mind that this summary won't apply to everyone.

For a more detailed look at the rules and how they may apply to your personal circumstances, you should get a copy of IRS Publication 590, *Individual Retirement Arrangements (IRAs)*.

These IRS publications and forms may also help:

- Publication 560, *Retirement Plans for the Self-Employed*
- Publication 571, *Tax-Sheltered Annuity Programs* (403(b) plans)
- Publication 575, *Pension and Annuity Income*
- Publication 939, *Pension General Rules*
- Form 5329, Additional Taxes Attributable to Qualified Retirement Plans including IRAs
- Form 5498, Individual Retirement Arrangement Information
- Form 8606, Nondeductible IRAs

For free copies, visit your local IRS office. Your public library may also have them available for reading or copying. You may also complete the order form in your tax package, or call the IRS at 1-800-TAX-FORM (1-800-829-3676).

If you have access to a computer, you may get copies by contacting the IRS's Web site at www.irs.ustreas.gov.

Planning
Your Estate

This chapter explores what happens to your IRA after you die; offers advice on picking a beneficiary, and on planning your estate matters in advance to reduce taxes and make life easier for your heirs; and looks at inheriting an IRA from the beneficiary's standpoint.

Traditional IRAs offer a lot of tax benefits while you're alive, but they can trigger tax complications after you die. That's why it's important to plan ahead so that you can avoid—or at least reduce—the tax impact on you and your beneficiaries.

Naming a Beneficiary

If there's any money left in your IRA when you die, who gets it is up to you. And one of the neat things about IRAs is that you get to name your own beneficiary. In this respect, then, IRAs can be a helpful tool for planning your estate.

You don't need a complex trust agreement, and you don't need to hire a lawyer. You just choose the person to whom you want the money to go. When you die, the assets in your IRA become the property of the beneficiary you named in your account papers.

It doesn't matter what your will says. It doesn't matter if you have no will. An IRA is a kind of "will substitute." In other words, your IRA generally doesn't have to go through the probate process—the procedure by which your will is "proven" in a court and your assets distributed under the court's supervision. If you have no will, a court oversees the distribution of your estate's assets according to the terms set by your state's laws.

The assets in your IRA, however, will pass automatically, by operation of law, directly to your beneficiary in much the same way that a life insurance policy's death benefit goes directly to the beneficiary.

An IRA, therefore, helps you avoid the potential delays, expense, and publicity that can accompany the probate process in some states. And you can name whomever you wish as your beneficiary. It doesn't have to be your spouse. It doesn't have to be an heir. You get to choose.

Complications When Choosing a Beneficiary

Just remember that there are big differences in taxes and other matters depending on whom you name as beneficiary. This is a complicated area that may well require the help of an accountant, financial planner, or similar professional, but below are a few general rules:

- You may not want to tap your IRA at all in retirement, perhaps because you have money from other sources, such as pensions and savings. As a result, you want to withdraw money from your IRA only as a last resort. Although the law requires you to start withdrawing at some point, you generally get to choose the method of withdrawal.
- In general, you can do the required calculation once and have it apply to all remaining withdrawals, or you can recalculate your life expectancy each year, which generally stretches out your withdrawals, thus keeping them smaller. If your spouse is your beneficiary, you may recalculate the life expectancies for both of you. This will generally keep the required annual withdrawals as small as possible. But if you name someone other than your spouse as beneficiary, you may only recalculate *your* life expectancy; recalculation isn't allowed for a nonspouse beneficiary. Choosing a nonspouse beneficiary therefore could mean you'll be required to make somewhat larger annual withdrawals. (This could boost your tax bill with less money left in your account each year to continue to grow tax deferred.)
- If your spouse is your beneficiary, he or she will have more flexibility as to what's done with your IRA's assets (and how they're taxed) after your death; a nonspouse beneficiary generally has far fewer options. One result is that a beneficiary who isn't your spouse may wind up paying income tax on your IRA far earlier than a spouse beneficiary would.
- If you don't have a beneficiary, your IRA will pass to your estate. In general, all the assets in your IRA will then have to be distributed to your heirs (based on your will, or on your state's laws if you have no will) within five years of your death.

Federal Estate Tax

Although your IRA may bypass probate court when you die, it may not escape federal estate taxes, sometimes called "death taxes."

If your estate is large enough, then the assets in your estate—including your IRAs—will be subject to the federal estate tax. The balances in your IRAs will be added to your estate in figuring any estate tax that's due. Most taxpayers don't have enough in assets to think about the estate tax, as we'll discuss in a moment.

If the value of your estate exceeds the threshold, however, you can reduce it—and therefore reduce or eliminate the tax—by earmarking some of your assets for charity. (Charitable donations escape the estate tax.)

Also, if you're married, any assets that are passed to your spouse—including your IRAs—will also escape the tax. In fact, if you earmark all your assets for your spouse, your estate will avoid the tax entirely. This is one reason you may want to name your spouse as your beneficiary.

Of course, your spouse's estate may be taxed in the future; it depends in part on its size, how the assets are arranged, and whether your spouse remarries. The 1997 tax law provided some relief by gradually increasing the total amount of assets you can have at your death before the estate tax is triggered.

Some Estate Tax Relief

For 1997 the first $600,000 of assets in an estate were generally exempt from the federal estate tax. Because of the 1997 Taxpayer Relief Act, the threshold will gradually increase over the years, until it reaches $1 million for 2006 and beyond. (See Figure 9.1.)

If your estate is likely to be taxed (or if your spouse's will after you die, and if you plan to pass your assets on to your spouse), you'll need to consult a financial planner, estate planning lawyer, or other professional adviser to help you map out some tax-saving strategies.

If, too, you've got the bulk of your assets tied up in IRAs or other retirement savings plans, you'll also have to make sure the rest of your estate has sufficient available liquid assets—cash or assets that can be quickly converted to cash—to cover tax, legal, administrative, funeral, and other expenses that will come due at your death. (Your lawyer, planner, accountant, or other adviser will also help you plan for any estate or inheritance taxes your state may levy.)

Figure 9.1   Avoiding the Federal Estate Tax

When you die, the assets that remain in your IRA(s) will be added to
your estate for purposes of figuring any federal estate tax due. If the
total value of an estate's assets falls below a certain dollar threshold,
the estate may escape the tax altogether. The threshold was $600,000,
but a new law passed in 1997 increases the threshold.

Year	Threshold
1997	$ 600,000
1998	625,000
1999	650,000
2000	675,000
2001	675,000
2002	700,000
2003	700,000
2004	850,000
2005	950,000
2006	1,000,000

Note: Technically, you're eligible for a "unified credit" that exempts assets from the federal unified estate and gift tax. For 1997 the credit of $192,800 sheltered $600,000 in assets from taxation.
A new law boosts the credit so that it shelters a greater amount of assets according to the schedule shown here. No provision has been made to increase the credit after 2006. (If a decedent has
an interest in certain types of family-owned businesses, other rules apply.)
Source: U.S. Congress

Elimination of Basis with IRAs

If you have a traditional *deductible* IRA, there is no tax basis in your
account. The entire value of the account, therefore, including your original
contributions plus any earnings, will be subject to federal income tax either
when you withdraw the money or when your beneficiary withdraws money
after you die.

If you have a traditional *nondeductible* IRA (discussed in full in Chapter
10), your account *will* have a basis for tax purposes that is equal to the amount
of after-tax dollars you contributed. When you die, that basis will be carried
over to your beneficiary; it won't be stepped up to the value of the account at
your death.

If, for example, you contributed $5,000 in after-tax dollars to a traditional nondeductible IRA and the account is worth $85,000 at your death, your beneficiary will have a carryover basis of $5,000. He or she won't have to pay income tax on the original $5,000 in contributions but *will* have to pay tax on any earnings the account has generated over the years. As a result, if the beneficiary were to withdraw the entire $85,000 after your death, he or she would have to pay federal income tax on $80,000.

This is an important point to keep in mind for your estate planning purposes. In general, the money in your traditional IRA will be taxed at some point, either when you withdraw it or when your beneficiary does. And while IRAs offer some tax benefits during your so-called wealth accumulation years—either through tax deductions for your contributions, tax deferral on your account earnings, or both—any withdrawals you make, or your beneficiary makes after you die, won't be eligible for favorable tax treatment.

Such withdrawals will be taxed as ordinary income. And it's possible that the assets in your IRA may wind up being taxed twice, according to two different tax systems: If your estate is large enough, your IRA could be subject to the federal estate tax; and the person who inherits your IRA will eventually wind up paying federal income tax on any withdrawals.

How soon withdrawals must be made and how long income tax may be deferred generally depend upon whom you name as your beneficiary and whether you die before or after you've started making the required minimum annual withdrawals.

What Triggers Income Tax

Federal income tax is triggered when money is withdrawn from an IRA. Thus, if you make withdrawals while you're alive, you must pay federal income tax for the year in which the withdrawal occurred.

There is some good news, however. First, if you're an IRA beneficiary, any amount you withdraw from an inherited IRA won't be slapped with the 10 percent early withdrawal penalty, no matter your age as the beneficiary and regardless of the age of the account owner at the time of death.

Another bit of good news is that you, as beneficiary of an inherited IRA, may be able to postpone withdrawals. This is really good news because if you don't need the money and can avoid withdrawing it, you'll avoid income tax and the money in the inherited IRA will continue to grow without being taxed each year.

The Beneficiary's Relationship with the IRA Owner

How long you, as a beneficiary, may postpone withdrawals from an inherited IRA depends in part on your relationship to the person who owned the IRA.

It also generally depends on whether the account's owner died before or after making required minimum withdrawals.

The rules for all this are fairly complicated, so if you're trying to plan ahead, talk with an estate lawyer, accountant, financial planner, or other financial adviser.

Here's a summary of how the rules work from the beneficiary's viewpoint:

Surviving spouse. If your spouse died and passed an IRA to you, you have far more options than another beneficiary would. For example, you may treat the inherited IRA as if it were your own. This means you may

- roll over the inherited IRA to your own IRA and thus postpone withdrawals until *you* turn 70½ and name your own beneficiary or beneficiaries; and
- contribute your own money to it or transfer (roll over) money to it.

If you choose not to treat the inherited IRA as your own, you generally must start withdrawing money from the IRA under either of these two options, whichever is later:

1. By December 31 of the year that your spouse would have reached 70½
2. By December 31 of the year *following* the year of your spouse's death

Let's take a closer look at your choices as the surviving spouse.

If you're the beneficiary and your spouse died *before* starting to make the required minimum annual withdrawals, you generally have several choices: withdraw the money in a lump sum immediately; withdraw it in stages (or in a lump sum) within five years after your spouse's death; make periodic withdrawals over your life expectancy; postpone withdrawals until your spouse would have turned 70½; or simply convert your spouse's IRA to your own IRA ("treat it as your own") and postpone withdrawals until *you* turn 70½ (and name your own beneficiary or beneficiaries).

If your spouse dies *after* starting the required minimum annual withdrawals, you may continue the withdrawals at the same pace as before or accelerate them, or simply convert or roll over the inherited IRA ("treat it as your own") and postpone withdrawals until you reach 70½.

As a general rule, you'll probably want to treat the inherited IRA as your own as that gives you the option to postpone withdrawals as long as possible. And as you know, by delaying withdrawals—perhaps for many years—you get to defer the payment of federal income tax on the IRA money you inherit. All the while, of course, the money in the IRA continues to grow on a tax-deferred basis.

Nonspouse beneficiary.   If you inherit an IRA from someone who is not your spouse, your options are limited. To the experts, this means you're a nonspouse beneficiary and thus can't treat the inherited IRA as your own. Therefore, you can't make contributions to it; you can't transfer or roll over money into it; and you can't roll over the inherited IRA itself into your own IRA.

What you *can* do is really a question of what you *must* do. If the owner dies *before* starting to make the required minimum annual withdrawals, you—as beneficiary—generally have two choices:

1. You must withdraw the *entire* balance of the IRA under the so-called five-year rule, which means you must pull out all the money in your inherited IRA by December 31 of the fifth year following the owner's death.
2. You must withdraw at least a minimum amount each year over your life expectancy, an option that could let you postpone making withdrawals far longer.

Whichever option you choose, you can't wait too long: You must make the choice by December 31 of the year following the owner's death. And this assumes that you have a choice: it's possible that the terms of the inherited IRA will require that you use one or the other option.

If you don't make a choice and your inherited IRA doesn't specify which rule you must follow, then you must—by default—pull out the entire balance within five years. In other words, the five-year rule applies.

If, however, you choose to make periodic withdrawals over your life expectancy (or if this option has been chosen for you under terms of your inherited IRA), then you must start withdrawing at least a minimum annual amount by December 31 of the year following the year that the account owner died.

If the Owner Has Begun Withdrawals

What if the owner dies *after* starting to make the required minimum annual withdrawals? In that case, you must continue making withdrawals at least as rapidly as called for under the method in use when the account owner died.

The bottom line? If you inherit an IRA and you're not the owner's surviving spouse, you don't have many choices. Within a fairly short time you've got to start withdrawing some—or all—of the account balance. And when you withdraw the money, you'll probably wind up paying income tax on it.

The Importance of Planning Ahead

As you can see, the rules governing IRAs give rise to a lot of tricky planning issues. For example, if your beneficiary isn't your spouse and doesn't have a lot of money, the beneficiary will face an unexpected income tax payment, which may have to be made shortly after you die. If the beneficiary doesn't have a lot of spare cash, he or she may have to tap into your IRA money—the inheritance—to pay the tax.

If you're the account owner, and you want to limit the income tax impact on your nonspouse beneficiary, you could take bigger withdrawals while you're alive. There'll be less money then left in the account after your death than there otherwise would be, but your nonspouse beneficiary would have less income tax to pay as well.

You could also take this strategy one step further: When you take bigger withdrawals while you're alive, you could gift some of the money to your nonspouse beneficiary. As long as you keep each gift to less than $10,000 per year (or $20,000 a year if you're married and your spouse agrees to the gift), there'll be no federal gift tax to pay; you reduce the size of your IRA for federal estate tax purposes; and your nonspouse beneficiary gets the gifts free of tax, because the recipient generally doesn't have to pay a federal tax for gifts he or she receives.

Leaving liquid assets in your estate. If your surviving spouse inherits your IRA, he or she may postpone withdrawing money—and delay the income tax consequences—for many years. If your IRA is your chief asset, however, your spouse may be forced to make withdrawals—and suffer tax consequences—if no other cash is available to pay your funeral and burial expenses, legal bills, final medical costs, and other expenses that arise as a result of your death.

For these and other reasons, it's a good idea for you to get expert help to put together a sound estate plan that can resolve thorny tax, legal, and other issues in advance of your death, including any state tax issues.

Helpful Hints

Here are some other points to keep in mind:

- If you made nondeductible contributions to your IRA (in other words, you contributed after-tax dollars to the account), the contributions won't be taxed when your beneficiary withdraws them. (But the beneficiary will have to use IRS Form 8606 to figure out which part of each withdrawal is and isn't taxable.)
- You have a general idea of how the government rules work for an IRA owner (and beneficiary) in making required minimum withdrawals and for a beneficiary (spouse or nonspouse) who inherits an IRA. But just because the government allows a lot of options doesn't necessarily mean your IRA trustee or custodian will also allow all these options. In some cases, your IRA trustee or custodian may have restrictions, giving you limited options. All this should be spelled out in the IRA disclosure document that you receive at the time you open an account.
- There may be reasons you don't want to inherit an IRA if you're the beneficiary; for example, you may not want to deal with the tax consequences. (There also may be important estate tax reasons for not wanting to accept an IRA.) If that's the case, you have the option to "disclaim" any interest in an IRA if you're the beneficiary. If you meet the many tricky rules in this area, you won't get any of the assets from the IRA, but you'll also avoid the income tax you would have had to pay. If you want to disclaim your rights to the assets in an IRA, consult with a lawyer.
- If you inherit an IRA, you may be able to claim a deduction on your tax return. Here's why: The owner's estate may have to pay estate tax for some of the IRA money that was paid out of the IRA on or about the time of the owner's death as "income in respect of a decedent." If that's the case, you may be able to claim an income tax deduction for the amount of the estate tax that was paid.
- If an IRA owner dies and there's more than one beneficiary, separate accounts may have to be set up for each beneficiary because each beneficiary may want to withdraw according to a different formula. For instance, if the account owner dies *after* minimum annual withdrawals had begun, one beneficiary may want to withdraw his or her share in a lump sum, but another beneficiary may want to withdraw her share in stages. Separate accounts allow each beneficiary his or her own choice.

To Sum Up . . .

As you know, IRAs offer a lot of flexibility when it comes to investment options and the ability to transfer your account from one custodian to another for example. Another area allowing flexibility is estate matters: You can pick whomever you like as beneficiary (you don't need anyone's permission for this), and when you die, your IRA will pass automatically by operation of law to your beneficiary, thus avoiding the probate process.

Choosing a beneficiary can be tricky because a lot hinges on your choice. Depending on whom you choose, for instance, you may have to make larger or smaller minimum required withdrawals while you're alive. Your choice of beneficiary may also help determine exactly how quickly the beneficiary must withdraw money from your account after he or she inherits it.

Although your IRA will bypass the probate process, it may not escape federal estate taxation. Whether it'll be subject to this tax depends, in part, on whom you pass the IRA to, the size of your estate, and other factors. Fortunately, fewer and fewer estates will be subject to the estate tax as the years pass because the government has changed the rules.

Nevertheless, when it comes to estate planning matters—with IRAs or other assets—practicing law or accounting on your own isn't a good idea. It's best to consult a professional who may be able to point out issues you weren't aware of and help you make plans that will reduce your taxes, ensure that there's enough liquidity in your estate to cover taxes and final expenses, and also make things easier on your heirs.

For More Information . . .

- Try one of the following books for more information on estate planning: *The Will Kit* by John Ventura; *Estate Planning Made Easy,* 2nd edition, by David T. Phillips and Bill Wolfkiel; or *Die Rich and Tax Free* by Barry Kaye. All can be found in your local bookstore or by calling Dearborn Financial Publishing at 1-800-245-2665.
- The IRS has booklets that offer details on issues related to death and taxes. One is Publication 559, *Tax Information for Survivors, Executors, and Administrators.* Another is Publication 950, *Introduction to Estate and Gift Taxes.* For your free copies, visit your local IRS office or public library, call the IRS at 1-800-TAX-FORM (1-800-829-3676), complete the order form in your income tax return package, or visit the IRS's Web site at www.irs.ustreas.gov.

Nondeductible IRAs

Nondeductible IRAs are still alive, and you need to know how they work either because you already own one or because you plan to open one (after having exhausted all other options). This chapter takes a look at the rules, including a plain-language guide to figuring what portion of your withdrawals will—and won't—be taxed.

Don't believe what you've heard about nondeductible IRAs. Reports of their death have been exaggerated.

They're still alive, they're still available, and their inner workings may interest you for two good reasons: either you have one of these accounts already, or you're considering opening one because you have nowhere else to turn.

Taxes Are Key

An IRA is nondeductible according to the nature of the contributions you make. The easiest way to understand it is to see how a nondeductible IRA compares with the traditional deductible IRA.

As you know by now, a deductible IRA has three main ingredients:

1. For every dollar you contribute, you may be able to claim a federal income tax deduction and thus cut your overall tax bill.
2. The money inside your account grows without being taxed each year.
3. Your original contributions and all your earnings will be taxed on withdrawal.

The nondeductible IRA is different in only one major way: you can't claim an income tax deduction for the money you contribute. (That's why it's called a "nondeductible" IRA: your contributions aren't deductible.) This, of course, means you won't get any immediate income tax benefit.

Why bother with a nondeductible? Even though you get no immediate tax benefit, the money that's in your account will still grow each year without being pinched by taxes. With nondeductible IRAs as well as with deductible IRAs, your money grows through the magic of tax-deferred compounding. That's a powerful feature. And that's what makes the nondeductible IRA potentially more appealing than some kinds of taxable accounts.

How a Nondeductible IRA Can Help

Suppose you put $2,000 a year in a nondeductible IRA and $2,000 a year in a taxable account, such as a savings account at your local bank. Just to keep things simple, let's also say that each account earns 5 percent a year in interest. After 20 years how much money will you have?

Here are the results, grouped according to federal income tax rates. Pick which marginal federal income tax rate applies to you:

15 percent bracket
$66,132 (nondeductible account)
$61,125 (taxable account)

36 percent bracket
$66,132 (nondeductible account)
$54,848 (taxable account)

28 percent bracket
$66,132 (nondeductible account)
$57,144 (taxable account)

39.6 percent bracket
$66,132 (nondeductible account)
$53,850 (taxable account)

31 percent bracket
$66,132 (nondeductible account)
$56,270 (taxable account)

The Flaw in a Nondeductible IRA

You may have spotted the flaw in the figures above. The comparisons don't tell the whole story. They show what happens when you put money *in*, but they don't show what happens when you take money *out*.

This is important: when you withdraw money from a nondeductible IRA, part of each withdrawal gets taxed as ordinary income. A portion of each withdrawal represents your original contributions, which you made with after-tax dollars (so they won't be taxed yet again). But the other portion of each withdrawal represents earnings, such as dividends, interest, and any price appreciation in your account over the years. These earnings *do* get taxed on withdrawal because they haven't been taxed before.

The Magic of Compounding

Even after taking taxes into account, you'd still be better off with the non-deductible IRA because your account has had the benefit of tax-deferred compounded growth over the years.

Let's look at our example again. If your income is taxed at the 28 percent marginal rate, your nondeductible IRA is worth $66,132 after 20 years. Now suppose you withdraw all that money from your nondeductible IRA. Of the total, $40,000 represents your original contributions (20 years times $2,000). It won't be taxed.

The remaining $26,132 represents earnings, and *will* be taxed, so you'll owe a federal tax of $7,317 in this example. After you pay the tax, you'll be left with $18,815 in earnings. Add back your original contributions of $40,000 and you'll net a total of $58,815 from your nondeductible IRA—even after paying tax.

Your net still beats the $57,144 that's left in your taxable account after 20 years. In other words, you'll have $1,671 *more* with the nondeductible IRA than with the taxable account in this example.

Even this doesn't tell the real story, however, because odds are you won't withdraw all the money from your nondeductible IRA in a lump sum. Instead, you'll probably pull the money out in installments, and this lets the balance keep growing on a tax-deferred basis. As a result, over the very long haul you'll be even better off with the nondeductible IRA. (The money in your taxable account will continue to grow, too, but it'll be taxed each year, so it won't grow as much as the nondeductible IRA.)

Advantages of Nondeductible IRAs

As you can see, the nondeductible IRA has its advantages and that's why some people have them. They don't beat traditional deductible IRAs, because with deductible IRAs you get an immediate federal income tax deduction for your contributions *plus* the benefit of tax-deferred compounded growth.

Some people don't qualify for deductible IRAs because their income is too high. They have few other options available to take advantage of tax-deferred growth, so they've chosen to use nondeductible IRAs.

Remember: Nondeductible IRAs are really just traditional IRAs with the key difference being whether your contributions are deductible or not. In general, if you're not covered by a pension plan at work, all your contributions to a regular IRA are deductible—that is, you can claim an income tax deduction for the amount you contribute. If you are covered by a pension plan at work, you can still contribute to an IRA, but whether your contributions are deductible depends on your income level. If your income is too high, your contributions to a regular IRA are nondeductible. You still have to have earned income—money from a job—to make nondeductible contributions to a traditional IRA.

Government statistics show that the use of nondeductible IRAs grew somewhat in the 1990s, indicating that at least some taxpayers were aware of their benefits. Because nondeductible IRAs have their own strange rules, it pays to know how the rules work if you own one.

How the Rules Work

Fortunately, the rules for nondeductible IRAs aren't all that different from the rules for traditional deductible IRAs. For instance, the most you can contribute each year to both is either $2,000 or the total of your earned income, whichever is less.

You have until April 15 to make a contribution to a nondeductible IRA for the previous year. If you do make a nondeductible contribution, you've got to let the government know about it, in detail, by filing IRS Form 8606 with your annual income tax return. (If you fail to file this form, you'll be subject to a $50 penalty.)

The government is actually doing you a favor by requiring you to file the form. The form will come in handy later on when it comes time to figure out how much of each withdrawal is tax-free and how much is taxable.

If you keep your forms on file—and you should—you'll have a convenient starting point from which to figure out the tax consequences for your withdrawals. You'll also have plenty of ammunition to fight the IRS in case your tax calculations are challenged.

Avoiding the Penalty

You generally can't withdraw money from a nondeductible or deductible IRA before you reach age 59½ because your earnings will be subject to income tax and you may face the 10 percent penalty on early withdrawals. (The same limited exceptions to the penalty that apply to deductible IRAs also apply to nondeductible IRAs: death, disability, installment payouts, and so on.)

If you withdraw money from a nondeductible IRA after you reach age 59½, you'll avoid the penalty altogether, but the earnings portion of each withdrawal will still be subject to federal income tax.

In addition, as with deductible IRAs, you can't leave your money in your account forever; the law generally requires that you begin making at least minimum annual withdrawals at about the time you reach age 70½.

A Different Formula

The formula you use to figure out how much of each withdrawal will be taxed is different from the formula for deductible IRAs because a portion of each withdrawal will represent a tax-free return of your original contributions. And you have to take this into account when you make your withdrawals.

The formula isn't all that hard, but it takes a little practice to get comfortable with it. Here, in a nutshell, is how it works.

Crunching the numbers.　You have to know a few important numbers—how much your account was worth before you made the withdrawal, how much in nondeductible contributions you made to the account over the years, and how much you're going to withdraw. Once you have these numbers, the calculation is fairly simple.

In essence, you use the numbers first to figure out what part of your account's overall value comes from nondeductible contributions. Whatever percentage that turns out to be is the percentage of your withdrawal that will be tax-free.

How the formula works.　Suppose, for example, that the total value of your nondeductible IRA is $20,000 before you make the withdrawal. You made a total of $2,000 in nondeductible contributions to your account over the years, and you now plan to withdraw $1,000.

What portion of that $1,000 withdrawal will be tax-free? What portion will be taxable?

Your total nondeductible contributions of $2,000 represent 10 percent of your overall account value of $20,000 ($2,000 divided by $20,000 equals 10 percent). As a result, 10 percent of your planned $1,000 withdrawal will be tax-free; the remainder will be subject to federal income tax at your marginal rate.

In this example, therefore, $100 of your $1,000 withdrawal will be tax-free (.10 times $1,000 equals $100). The rest of your withdrawal—$900 in this example—will be taxed as ordinary income. If your marginal tax rate is 28 percent, therefore, you'll owe $252 in tax for this withdrawal (.28 times $900).

Here's another way to look at it: Of your $1,000 withdrawal, you'll wind up paying $252 in federal tax and you'll be left with $748.

A handy sketch.   The government supplies worksheets that you may use to figure out the tax consequences of withdrawals from a nondeductible IRA, but you can sketch it out yourself with a simple formula:

Nondeductible contributions ÷ Prewithdrawal account value
× Amount of your withdrawal = Tax-free portion of your withdrawal

Using the numbers in our example, here's how the formula would look:

$$\$2,000 \div \$20,000 \times \$1,000 \ = \ \$100$$

This formula can get a bit more complicated if you've also made deductible contributions to the same account. To avoid the added complexity, you might want to have one IRA devoted entirely to nondeductible contributions and one or more other IRAs devoted entirely to your deductible contributions. This can make the paperwork—and the calculations—a bit easier at tax time.

When a Nondeductible IRA Can Help

Although nondeductible IRAs require some extra paperwork and some extra figuring, they still have value. And if you don't qualify for a fully deductible IRA contribution, remember that you can still make nondeductible contributions.

Suppose, for example, that you're covered by a pension plan at work. Suppose, too, that because you have a certain amount of adjusted gross income, you're allowed only a $1,500 deductible IRA contribution. (In other words, the amount of the deduction you may claim is "phased out" because of your income level.)

If that's the case, keep in mind that your annual limit on IRA contributions overall is still $2,000. So in this example you may still contribute a full $2,000 to your IRA for the year (assuming, of course, that you had at least $2,000 in earned income or "taxable compensation" for the year and that you're under 70½). But you'll get a federal income tax deduction for only $1,500 of the contribution; the remaining $500 will count as a nondeductible contribution.

If you make the $500 nondeductible contribution, you'll have to file a special form along with your federal income tax return. And to help minimize accounting complications, you may want to put the $500 in a separate account.

Considering Your Options

If you're eligible to contribute to a tax-favored retirement savings plan at work, such as a 401(k) or 403(b) plan, do it. It's a much better option than a nondeductible IRA. You get an up-front tax deduction for the amount you contribute to 401(k) and 403(b) plans. Your money usually is set aside through payroll deductions, a convenient way to save. And your employer may kick in some money to your account as an incentive for you to save. You may also have the option to borrow against your account depending on the plan and on your company's rules.

Among IRAs, the traditional deductible IRA beats the nondeductible IRA for most taxpayers. You get an up-front income tax deduction (depending on your income level) and your account grows tax deferred. (Withdrawals are subject to tax and possible penalty.)

The Roth IRA's Edge

The Roth IRA is also an attractive alternative. (For more on Roth IRAs, see Chapter 12.) True, you can't claim an income tax deduction for the amount you contribute to Roth IRAs as well as nondeductible IRAs. But there's also a key difference.

With the nondeductible IRA, earnings grow on a *tax-deferred* basis, which means the earnings in your account aren't taxed each year, although they'll be taxed when they're withdrawn. With the Roth IRA, however, earnings grow *tax-free*. As long as you meet the rules, all your withdrawals are entirely free of federal tax. This is one reason it makes a lot of sense to convert existing nondeductible IRAs to Roth IRAs. (For more on conversions, see Chapter 13.)

Why Congress Retains Nondeductibles

When Congress adopted sweeping changes to the federal tax code in 1997, it specifically mentioned that nondeductible IRAs would continue to exist, even though they are no longer a practical option for most taxpayers. Why bother with a nondeductible IRA at all?

If you aren't eligible for an up-front income tax deduction with the traditional IRA because your income is too high, then the traditional IRA becomes, in effect, a nondeductible IRA.

With the Roth IRA, you can't contribute unless your income is below a certain level. If you're single, you may make a full contribution if your adjusted gross income is below $95,000; a partial contribution on income between $95,000 and $110,000; and no contribution above that. If you're married and filing jointly, you may make a full contribution if your adjusted gross income is below $150,000; a partial contribution on income between $150,000 and $160,000; and no contribution above that.

As you can see, some taxpayers are allowed only a partial contribution to Roth IRAs; and some can't contribute at all. If you can't make a full $2,000 annual contribution to a Roth ($4,000 for married couples filing jointly) and you still want to set aside some money in an IRA, consider the nondeductible IRA. It's still an option if only for a much smaller number of taxpayers than before. (Remember: The overall annual contribution limit to IRAs is $2,000, which applies across the board to traditional deductible IRAs, nondeductible IRAs, and Roth IRAs. Education IRAs, discussed in Chapter 11, aren't included in this across-the-board limit.)

To Sum Up . . .

Nondeductible IRAs aren't dead, so it's worth understanding how they work, either because you already have one or because you plan to open one after exhausting all your other options.

Nondeductible IRAs, however, probably won't be as appealing as they once were. If you don't qualify for a traditional deductible IRA but you still want to set some money aside in an IRA, you'll have to contribute after-tax dollars. The best IRA for after-tax contributions is the Roth IRA, but some people won't qualify for the Roth because their income is too high. Thus, the nondeductible IRA is really an IRA of last resort.

For More Information . . .

If you own a nondeductible IRA already, or if you're planning to open one, you must have a copy of IRS Form 8606, *Nondeductible IRAs (Contributions, Distributions, and Basis)*. You use this form to figure out not only your annual contributions but also how much of each withdrawal is taxable.

You must also keep a copy of this form as proof, should the IRS question you, of why a certain part of each withdrawal is tax-free.

To get your own free copy, visit your local IRS office or public library, call the IRS at 1-800-TAX-FORM (1-800-829-3676), or visit the IRS's Web site at www.irs.ustreas.gov.

The Education IRA

The education IRA is a new way to save for a child's college education. But is it your best option? This chapter looks at how the education IRA works, who's eligible, who isn't, the benefits and drawbacks of investing in this account, and which alternatives are best.

The education IRA is an individual retirement account that has nothing to do with retirement. Even though its name includes the initials *IRA*, it's *not* an IRA. Instead, it's a kind of savings account that offers tax benefits if you set aside money to help pay for a child's (or grandchild's) college education.

Here, in a nutshell, is how it works. Once you set up an education IRA—at a bank, brokerage, or mutual fund company, for example—you may contribute up to $500 in cash each year per child. If you have more than one child or grandchild, therefore, you can have more than one education IRA.

When the time is right, you withdraw the money to help pay for a child's or grandchild's college expenses. You don't get an income tax deduction for the amount you contribute, but the earnings inside the account grow each year without being taxed. And if the money is used for college education expenses, the withdrawals are entirely free of tax and penalty.

Is It a Good Idea?

Before getting into all the details, ask one important question: Is this account a good idea for you? Not necessarily. The tax benefits make it tempting, it's true, and the maximum amount that can be contributed on behalf of a child—$500 a year—makes it even more attractive for some people. Even if you don't already have some money set aside for a child's or grandchild's college education, odds are you can probably scrape together $500 over a year's time to salt away for this purpose.

Figure 11.1   The Education IRA at a Glance

Some highlights of the education IRA:

- You contribute after-tax dollars with no deductions allowed.
- The maximum contribution is $500 per year per child.
- Contributions are allowed until the child is 18.
- Anyone may contribute, such as parents, grandparents, family friends, and relatives.
- Full contribution is allowed only if your adjusted gross income is less than $95,000 (if single) or $150,000 (if married filing jointly). Above these limits, the contribution is reduced or not allowed depending on your income level.
- Withdrawals are tax-free and penalty-free if used for such higher-education expenses as tuition, fees, books, supplies, and equipment.
- If the account balance remains when the child is 30, the money must be withdrawn and taxed to the beneficiary, but tax may be avoided if the balance is moved to an education IRA of another family member.

Source: Congressional Conference Committee Report

In fact, the same law that created the education IRA also created new income tax credits that can be claimed each year by eligible families for each child they have. The credit amounted to $400 per child for 1998 and rose to $500 per child for 1999 and later years. Some parents may look at it this way: We're going to get an income tax refund this year because of Junior, so we'll deposit that money in an education IRA on Junior's behalf.

In other words, the education IRA—and its $500 annual limit on contributions—can give a parent or grandparent a good excuse to start saving. And there's nothing wrong with that.

A Few Problems

There are nonetheless some problems with the education IRA, as you'll see in more detail later in this chapter. For now, here are some highlights:

- The same thing that might attract certain people to the education IRA—its $500 limit—may turn other people off. Smart investors know that saving $500 a year over 18 years probably won't be enough to pay for a child's college expenses. In fact, it might not be enough to pay for even a year's worth of expenses, so maybe the education IRA is merely a starting point or a supplement. (See Figure 11.2.) And for all the rules

Figure 11.2   Saving with the Education IRA

Because annual contributions are limited, you can't save much with
the education IRA. Still, by saving $500 a year, the money can add up,
offering a helpful supplement to a broader savings plan.

	After 5 Years	After 10 Years	After 18 Years
At 5%	$2,763	$6,289	$14,066
At 8%	2,933	7,243	18,725
At 10%	3,053	7,969	22,800
At 12%	3,176	8,774	27,875

Note: These figures assume that $500 is invested at the end of each year. Depending on how the
IRS rules, you may be allowed to contribute for up to 19 years if contributions begin at the child's
birth and end at the child's 18th birthday.

you must learn and all the other hurdles and complications involved, is
the education IRA worth the trouble as a side dish only and not the
main meal?

- For some people (including me!), $500 is a lot of money, but if you're
  the head of a giant bank, brokerage, or mutual fund company, $500 is
  peanuts. For this reason, some outfits that normally offer IRAs might
  not also offer the education IRA because by their standards, it's a small
  account. The money these organizations can make from such small
  accounts may not be enough to offset their mailing, recordkeeping and
  other expenses. As a result, you may not have as many investment
  choices with an education IRA as you'd like because not every institution will offer it.
- Although education IRAs are a little less complicated than traditional
  IRAs, *they're still complicated.* If you want to open one, you'll have to
  learn how it works. The education IRA has its own set of rules and regulations, and not all details have been set yet by the IRS. (In fairness,
  the accounts are fairly new. They were created by the Taxpayer Relief
  Act of 1997 and were allowed for the first time in January 1998.) Open
  one up and you're bound to invite a flood of account statements,
  account reports, and tax statements from the trustee or custodian. Do
  you need all this extra paperwork and worry?
- The most that can be contributed in any one year is $500 per benefi-
  ciary. Maybe that's all you can afford. But who's going to keep track of
  all the friends and relatives who may also want to contribute to an education IRA each year on behalf of a single child? You? Your spouse?
  Your in-laws?

Understanding the Tax Breaks

Even if you're not interested in opening an education IRA for a child, odds are that someone else has probably already mentioned these accounts to you. It helps to know what it is and how it works.

First, the tax breaks. In some ways, education IRAs are more like the new Roth IRAs than traditional IRAs. (For more on Roth IRAs, see the following chapter.) For instance, you can't claim an income tax deduction for the money you contribute, but the money does grow on a tax-favored basis. In other words, all the money your education IRA earns each year—whether it's in the form of interest, dividends, or capital gains—doesn't get nicked by the tax man every year, as it would if it you had set the money aside in a bank account or in certain types of brokerage or mutual fund accounts. And when you withdraw the money, it doesn't get taxed as long as you meet the rules.

Some of the rules get a little tricky, especially if you try to use the education IRA when you're trying to take advantage of other education savings programs at the same time.

Income Limits

Before you can open an education IRA, you've got to consider income limits. Because the government wants education IRAs to be used mainly by lower-income and middle-income people, whether you can contribute depends on your income:

- If you're single and your adjusted gross income (AGI) is less than $95,000, you may contribute the full $500 per year per child. If your AGI is between $95,000 and $110,000, you may make partial contributions. If your AGI is $110,000 or more, you can't contribute at all.
- If you're married and filing jointly, and your AGI is less than $150,000, you may contribute the full $500 per child. If your AGI is between $150,000 and $160,000, you may make partial contributions. If it's $160,000 or more, you can't make any contributions.

Keep in mind that these income limits apply to the person contributing the money, not to the beneficiary. But unlike with a traditional IRA, you don't need to have earned income (from a job) in order to contribute to an education IRA; your beneficiary doesn't need to have earned income either.

Limits on the Type of School

Because the education IRA is kind of like a trust or custodial account that you set up to help pay for a child's postsecondary education, you can't spend the money to send the child to a private elementary school or high school. But you *can* use it to send a child to a college or university.

The student can use the money for study either at the undergraduate or graduate level. And the money can be used for lots of things, not just tuition and fees, but also for books, supplies, equipment, and room and board.

What's more, it generally doesn't matter if the child is a full-time or part-time student. But if you're using the money to pay normal room-and-board expenses, the student must be enrolled on at least a half-time basis.

As long as you meet these rules, money that's withdrawn from an education IRA won't be taxed. Period. No federal income taxes. No federal penalties. No "age 59½" rule or any of the other complex rules that traditional IRAs usually have.

Cashing In on the Benefits

What does the absence of traditional IRA rules mean to your pocketbook? Say you set aside $500 in an education IRA each year for ten years. The account earns 8 percent a year. In the end, you will have saved about $7,243, which includes $5,000 of original contributions plus earnings of about $2,243.

If you didn't use an education IRA, but instead used some sort of taxable account, the $2,243 in earnings in this example would be taxed. Exactly how it would be taxed would depend on the type of account you had and on your tax bracket. In general, though, your federal income tax bill on these earnings might amount to about $336 if you were in the 15 percent tax bracket or $628 if you were in the 28 percent bracket.

On the other hand, if you meet all the rules for the education IRA, none of the $2,243 in earnings would be taxed. (And because your original investment of $5,000 was made with after-tax dollars, it wouldn't be taxed again.) So you—or your beneficiary—would potentially save hundreds of income tax dollars.

In essence, that saving is the beauty of the education IRA. The government is saying that if you use one of these accounts to save money for your child's college education and you meet all the rules, then the money that your account has earned over the years can escape taxation altogether. Or, put another way, the federal government is willing to underwrite part of your child's college education for you.

Obey the Limits

To be eligible, you have to meet all the rules—and there are a lot of them. For instance, you may contribute money to an education IRA on a child's behalf only until the child reaches age 18.

, The money from the account must be used for the kind of expenses mentioned earlier. Also, the annual contribution limit, you'll recall, is $500 per child per year. You may therefore have more than one education IRA per child, but no more than $500 per year can be contributed overall—from all sources—on behalf of a single child.

The $500 limit isn't indexed to rise each year with inflation (just as the $2,000 annual contribution limit for other IRAs isn't indexed to inflation). The $500 limit will stay at $500 a year unless Congress does something about it in the future.

When It's Time to Withdraw

If you're the beneficiary of an education IRA (in other words, if you're the student for whom the account is intended to benefit), what happens if your education IRA provides you with more than enough money to cover higher-education costs?

In such a case, you'll generally have to report the excess as income, making it subject to taxation. In general, though, you'll only be taxed on the amount that exceeds the basis in the account. In other words, you won't be taxed on the contributions that were made to your education IRA because these contributions were made with after-tax dollars (no income tax deduction was allowed).

The IRS provides a formula a beneficiary must use to figure out how much will and will not be taxed. It has to do with the relationship between the amount of expenses and the amount of the withdrawal.

A congressional committee report, issued at about the time the 1997 tax law was approved, offered this example: The student pulls $1,000 out of his or her education IRA in a given year, including $600 of principal (original contributions) and $400 of earnings (accumulated interest and dividends, for example). For that year, the student has $750 in college expenses.

How will the tax work? Again, the reason has to do with the relationship between the amount of expenses and the amount of the withdrawal. In this instance, the expenses account for 75 percent of the withdrawal ($750 of expenses is 75 percent of the $1,000 withdrawal).

Thus, 75 percent of the $400 in earnings will avoid tax, but 25 percent of it won't. Of the $400 in earnings, the student will get to *exclude* from his or her income 75 percent of it ($300) and *include* in income 25 percent of it (or $100).

The Closing Bell

What if there's still money left over in the education IRA when the student graduates? The money can't stay in there forever because the law requires it be pulled out before the beneficiary reaches age 30. At that point, the beneficiary will have to report the earnings as income, making it subject to taxation. The beneficiary will also have to pay a 10 percent penalty on the earnings.

A big exception to this rule, however, can be used to avoid taxation altogether. It involves rollovers and here's how it works. Suppose there's still money left in the education IRA even after the beneficiary has graduated and no longer needs it. To avoid taxation, the money may be rolled over, or transferred, to *another* education IRA that's set up to benefit another member of the beneficiary's family.

Suppose you have two sons, Dean and Riley, and you set up education IRAs for each of them. You've used some of the money in Dean's account to help pay for his college costs. After Dean graduates, there's still money left in his account. Dean can transfer the money to Riley's account, tax-free, where it can be used to help pay for Riley's college costs now or later.

Will It Work for You?

Now that you have an idea how the education IRA works, the key question is whether it'll work for you. To answer that, you have to look at a lot of different angles.

First, there's a practical matter to think about. As mentioned earlier, all the institutions that usually offer traditional IRAs may not offer education IRAs because the education accounts are bound to be small, and it costs money to service small accounts.

A bank, mutual fund, or brokerage firm may charge an annual fee to offset service costs, but a fee would really eat into the amount your account could earn. Suppose, for example, that you set up an education IRA at a bank and decide to plunk the full $500 into the account, earning 5 percent a year.

By the end of the first year the account might be worth about $525. But if the bank charges you a $10 annual account maintenance or servicing fee, then 40 percent of what your account earned in this example will have been eaten up by fees. The bank might let you pay the $10 fee separately instead of taking the money out of the account, but that's ten extra dollars you'd have to kick in out-of-pocket.

More Points to Consider

Other points that could have an even bigger effect on your pocketbook must be considered. For example:

- If you use money from an education IRA to help pay for a child's college education in a given year, you can't also claim the Hope Scholarship Credit for that year. The Hope Credit, which took effect in January 1998, is valuable because it generally lets you claim a tax credit of up to $1,500 per student per year for tuition and related expenses during the first two years of college. A credit is important because it cuts your overall income tax bill dollar for dollar. If your federal tax liability is $5,000 for a given year and you qualify for a $1,500 tax credit, your tax bill would be slashed by $1,500, to $3,500 in this example. And if you'd already paid the $5,000 tax (through payroll withholding at work, for example), you'll get a $1,500 income tax refund.
- If you use the education IRA to pay for a child's college expenses, you can't also take advantage of the Lifetime Learning Credit in the same year. This, too, means big bucks. The Lifetime Learning Credit, for college expenses paid after June 30, 1998 (for education beginning after that date), generally allows you a tax credit of up to $1,000 a year through 2002. And the credit limit rises to $2,000 for 2003 and later years. (You can't take advantage of both the Hope Credit *and* the Lifetime Learning Credit; it's one or the other.)
- It also isn't entirely clear how the financial aid people will view the education IRA. If it's viewed as part of a student's assets, the student might not receive as much in financial aid as he or she might if the account were viewed as part of your assets.
- In any given year, you can't contribute to an education IRA on a child's behalf if you contribute to a state-sponsored college tuition program for the same child.

Because the disadvantages may outweigh the benefits in many cases, the education IRA may work best only as a supplement to a broader savings plan. In other words, you should first check out better, more flexible alternatives and fund an education IRA only after exhausting those alternatives.

Is an Education IRA Enough?

Even if you were to fully fund an education IRA each year, odds are you'd fall short of covering a major portion of a child's total college education costs. For example, if you were able to invest $500 a year for 18 years in an education IRA and you earned an average of 8 percent a year, you'd wind up with about $18,725. For some schools, that wouldn't even pay the first year's bill.

Think about it. For the 1997–98 school year, the average total cost of tuition, fees, books, supplies, room and board, transportation, and other expenses for attending just one year at a four-year public college or university was $10,069, according to The College Board, an association of colleges and universities that compiles such figures. And for a four-year private college or university, the total average cost of just one year's education was $21,424.

Those figures are for a single year, the 1997–98 school year. What'll the numbers look like in the future? Nobody knows for sure, of course. But if you used the 1997–98 figures as a base and increased them based on an average annual college-cost inflation rate of 5 percent a year, you'd find that the total average cost of a single year's education for the 2015–16 school year would be about $24,232 at a public school and $51,560 at a private school.

Your child's college bill may not be that high. He or she may decide to commute instead of rooming in. Or maybe the child will wind up in a two-year school, such as a community college, where expenses are typically far less. There are lots of other ways to cut down on college expenses too. The point is that the education IRA alone may not be able to do the trick.

Consider the Alternatives

Let's look at some alternatives to the education IRA. For instance, you may now withdraw money penalty-free from a regular IRA, regardless of your age, to pay for college education expenses.

If you have a traditional IRA to which you have made deductible contributions over the years, you may withdraw money from that IRA even before you've reached age 59½ and pay no premature withdrawal penalty—if the money is used for college costs. (You'll still have to report the amount of your withdrawal as income, making it subject to federal income tax as well as state income tax where applicable, but you won't have to pay a penalty.)

If you withdraw money from a nondeductible IRA, only the earnings will be taxed, but they won't be penalized if used to pay for college expenses. (For more about nondeductible IRAs, see Chapter 10.)

The Roth IRA.   The Roth IRA can also be a far superior alternative to the education IRA. More details on Roth IRAs are in the following chapter, but, in general, you may contribute up to $2,000 a year to a Roth account, which is $1,500 *more* per year than the education IRA allows.

Roth withdrawals are completely free of federal taxation and penalty *if* the account has been in existence for five taxable years *and* if they're made

- after you reach age 59½;
- because you're disabled;
- on account of your death; or
- for first-time homebuyer expenses.

If you withdraw money from your Roth account and you don't meet the requirements listed here, what happens? If you withdraw only your original contributions, they won't be taxed. One strategy therefore might be to contribute each year to a Roth account, then pull out only your original contributions to pay for college expenses and leave the earnings to continue to grow toward another long-term goal, such as retirement.

What if you do wind up withdrawing the entire amount from your Roth account to pay for college costs? Only the account's earnings that you withdraw will be taxed. Ordinarily, they'd also be subject to a 10 percent federal penalty, but any earnings that you withdraw under these circumstances will avoid the penalty entirely if they're used to pay for education expenses.

Let's say you invest $2,000 a year for 18 years at 8 percent a year in a Roth account. You'd wind up with about $75,000. Of that total, $36,000 is from your original contributions (18 years times $2,000).

Under the Roth rules, you could withdraw the $36,000 to pay a student's college education costs without incurring any federal income tax or penalty because the withdrawal represents only your original contributions.

The $39,000 in earnings might also escape tax and penalty if they were withdrawn under the right circumstances (if you were older than 59½ or you were disabled, for example). If you didn't qualify under these exceptions, the $39,000 in earnings would be taxed if withdrawn, but they wouldn't also be penalized if you used the money for college costs.

You could always leave the earnings in the account for as long as you wanted because you never have to make withdrawals from a Roth IRA—ever. (Education IRAs and regular IRAs generally require that withdrawals be made—or start to be made—at some point.)

Other Choices

A lot of other investment options you may use to save for a child's college education, including regular taxable accounts, are available. You wouldn't enjoy the sort of tax benefits you'd get from an IRA, but you'd have a lot of flexibility with none of the restrictions imposed by IRA rules.

Say you set aside $2,000 a year for 18 years in a mutual fund whose performance is linked to some sort of broad stock market index, such as the Standard & Poor's index of 500 blue chip stocks. And say the account grows an average of 10 percent a year. You might wind up with a total of about $91,200 in your account.

If you cashed out and paid federal capital gains taxes on the increase in value of your mutual fund shares over the years, you might end up with about $86,800 (depending on your tax bracket), and that kind of money could make a big dent in college costs.

Here's how it would work: The $91,200 balance in your mutual fund account in this example would include $36,000 from your original investments ($2,000 a year times 18 years). Because those annual investments are made with your after-tax dollars, they won't be taxed again when you cash out.

The $91,200 balance in your fund account would also include about $55,200 in growth (from the increase in the market value of your fund's shares). That money *is* taxable, but you might have to pay federal capital gains tax on this money at a rate of only 8 percent if you were otherwise in the 15 percent federal income tax bracket. (Remember: If you're normally in the 15 percent bracket, the long-term capital gains rate you pay now on the profit from the sale of shares of stock or mutual funds is 10 percent. In 2001 and later, it drops to just 8 percent for assets held at least five years.)

After paying a federal tax of about $4,416 in our example, you'd be left with about $50,800 on the growth portion alone. Add back the amount of your original annual investments—$36,000 in our example—and you'd net about $86,800 after taxes.

As this example makes clear, investing in stocks, mutual funds, or other such assets can also be an effective way to save for long-term goals, such as a college education, even after paying taxes.

To Sum Up . . .

Here's a summary look at the education IRA.

Advantages:

- It provides flexible investment options. You may open an education IRA with any bank, brokerage, mutual fund, or insurance company that offers education IRAs, and money can be invested in just about anything.
- You may contribute on behalf of any child; the beneficiary need not be related to you.

- The account grows on a tax-deferred basis, so earnings aren't taxed each year.
- The account may be transferred, or rolled over, from one trustee to another, so you're not locked into your original trustee or custodian.
- Withdrawals are entirely tax-free if used to pay for the student's tuition, fees, and related expenses.
- Families with more than one child may set up and contribute to an education IRA for each child.
- If the account still has a balance after the student graduates, the money may be transferred, without tax consequence, to another family member's education IRA.

Disadvantages:

- Your ability to contribute is limited by your income. Full annual contributions are allowed only if your adjusted gross income is less than $95,000 for a single taxpayer, or less than $150,000 for married taxpayers filing jointly.
- Contributions aren't tax deductible.
- Once you contribute, you can't get the money back; it must be used on the beneficiary's behalf and only for postsecondary education expenses.
- Annual contributions are limited to $500 a year per beneficiary. (A 6 percent penalty applies to excess contributions.)
- The amount in the beneficiary's account may be counted against him or her when financial aid is calculated.
- No contributions are allowed after the beneficiary reaches age 18.
- The entire account balance must be withdrawn by the beneficiary's 30th birthday. (It may be transferred to another family member's education IRA.)
- If withdrawals aren't used for higher-education expenses and the money isn't transferred to an education IRA for another family member by the beneficiary's 30th birthday, the beneficiary will have to report the balance in the account as income, making it subject to federal income tax. The beneficiary also will face a 10 percent penalty.

For More Information . . .

Here are some resources you may use to get more information about saving for college:

- The Institute of Certified Financial Planners in Denver has a brochure that outlines ways you can save for a child's college education. To read the brochure, contact the group's Web site at www.icfp.org.
- The Vanguard Group of mutual funds has a more detailed 30-page booklet that offers tips on investing to help pay for college. It also lists potential sources of financial aid and includes worksheets to help you calculate how much a college education will cost and how much you'll have to save to cover the expense. In addition, the booklet reviews the impact of tax law changes on your savings strategies, including the education IRA, the Hope Scholarship Credit, the Lifetime Learning Credit, and deductions for interest on student loans. For your free copy of *Financing College: Planning for Your Child's Education*, call 1-800-662-7447, or write: Vanguard, P.O. Box 2600, Valley Forge, PA 19482. In addition, Vanguard's Web site now has an interactive electronic worksheet that parents may use to calculate whether their current investment program will be enough to pay for college costs. Contact the site at www.vanguard.com.
- If you're doing tax planning involving education, the IRS has issued special guidance that offers details on how tax rules work for the Hope Scholarship Credit; Lifetime Learning Credit; deductions for student loan interest; education IRAs; tapping regular or Roth IRAs penalty-free to pay for college; employer-provided educational assistance; and tax rules for state-sponsored prepaid tuition programs. The details are contained in IRS Notice 97-60, a thorough and well-written guide that includes a lot of information in an easy-to-read question-and-answer format. It's written for the consumer, not the tax professional. You may be able to get a copy at your local public library; or, if you have access to a computer, you may read or download a copy by contacting the IRS's Web site at www.irs.ustreas.gov. Or call the IRS at 1-800-829-3676 and ask for Publication 3064, and a related booklet, Publication 970.

The Roth IRA

This chapter looks beyond the hype to see how the Roth IRA works and whether it'll work for you; it reviews the Roth's tax and other benefits and compares the Roth IRA with a regular IRA and other investments.

There's a bright new star in the IRA galaxy called the Roth IRA. Don't start reading yet. Go out and open a Roth IRA first.

It's that good. In fact, it's great. The Roth IRA is simply a splendid way to save. So don't waste another moment. Go and open an account, and contribute the maximum—$2,000—this year and every year.

What's the big deal? The Roth IRA isn't really an IRA at all. It's more a savings account than a retirement account. But it's a super-duper savings account, one that offers all sorts of delightful benefits. And you should take advantage of it as soon as you can.

A Quick Look at the Benefits

In a way, Congress modeled the Roth IRA after the old, traditional IRA, but they're so very different that it's hard to imagine they came from the same family.

When it created the Roth IRA, for instance, Congress stripped away one of the sweetest benefits that the traditional IRA offers—your ability to claim a federal income tax deduction for the amount you contribute. Score one for the traditional IRA.

In creating the Roth IRA, however, Congress also scrapped some of the worst features of the traditional IRA. With the Roth IRA, for example, your withdrawals won't be taxed or penalized at all as long as you meet the rules. (With traditional IRAs, withdrawals are almost always taxable and may be penalized, too.)

No Required Withdrawals

What's more, there's no requirement whatsoever to withdraw any money at all from a Roth IRA. There's no need then to start fretting when you turn 70½, no need to grind through all of the tables and formulas that come with making the required minimum withdrawals from a traditional IRA.

As a result, you can leave all your money in your Roth account if you so choose and just pass it along to the next generation. And your beneficiaries generally will be able to withdraw money tax-free from the Roth account that they inherit from you.

You want to contribute to a Roth IRA *after* you turn 70½? Feel free. You won't have to stop making contributions just because of your age as you do with a traditional IRA. Score one more for the Roth IRA. In fact, score lots for the Roth IRA because it's simply an incredible way to save money.

Yes, there are some rules to think about. (This wouldn't be an IRA if there weren't a lot of details.)

Yes, a regular taxable account might give you more flexibility. (But you won't get the benefits that the Roth account offers.)

Yes, there are income limits to think about too. (As a result, people with high incomes won't be eligible.)

And yes, Congress could change the rules some day. (That's true with any law.)

But skip all that for now and just take the plunge because it's hard to imagine a better deal than the Roth IRA.

A Look at the Details

What exactly is a Roth IRA? How, precisely, does it work? The answer is pretty simple. It has to do with taxes. When you contribute money to a Roth IRA, you get no immediate tax benefit, as you know. But the money that's inside your Roth IRA will grow year after year without being taxed. And when you withdraw the money, it doesn't get taxed then either if you meet the rules.

That's the summary. The details: to understand the benefits of a Roth IRA, first think about how the traditional IRA usually operates. When you contribute money to a traditional IRA, you may get a federal income tax deduction.

In other words, for the amount of money you contribute, you may be able to deduct an equal amount on your federal income tax return. This, in effect, means you may be able to report to the government less money than you actually earned. As a result, you may wind up paying less income tax than you ordinarily would.

The Magic of Compound Interest

The traditional IRA has another key tax benefit. As the value of your IRA grows over time, the growth doesn't get taxed. As a result, all the interest, dividends, and the increase in price of whatever is inside your IRA—whether stocks, bonds, or mutual funds, for example—grows year after year without being nicked by the tax man. The only time that the money in your traditional IRA *is* taxed is when you take it out.

The Roth IRA works like a traditional IRA in some ways but not in others. One big difference is that the money you contribute to a Roth IRA is *not* tax deductible. You get no up-front tax break by contributing to a Roth IRA, although as the value of your Roth IRA grows over the years, the growth, like that with a traditional IRA, isn't taxed.

The Key Benefit Comes at the End

The really big difference between traditional IRAs and Roth IRAs comes at the end. As long as you meet the rules, the money you withdraw from a Roth IRA comes out free of tax.

That's the real beauty of the Roth IRA. With the traditional IRA, your withdrawals are taxable (to the extent you withdraw original *deductible* contributions and earnings; *nondeductible* contributions aren't taxed when withdrawn). Also, the withdrawals get taxed as ordinary income, so the higher your income tax bracket, the higher the tax on your withdrawals.

With the Roth IRA, however, there is no tax. Your money grows tax-free while it's in your account, and it comes out tax-free when you withdraw it.

Experts call the Roth IRA "back-loaded" or "back-ended" because important tax benefits come at the end. (You may also have heard it described as the IRA Plus or American Dream IRA, but a joint congressional committee changed the name of the account at the last minute to honor its creator, Republican Senator William V. Roth Jr. of Delaware, the tireless champion of IRAs who is also chairman of the Senate Finance Committee.)

One of the main reasons Roth IRAs are getting so much attention is not just as an alternative to traditional IRAs but also as an alternative to most types of taxable investments.

Want to put your money in a regular bank account? The interest you earn will be taxed, year after year, and it'll be taxed as ordinary income. Do you prefer to put your money in stocks or stock mutual funds instead? If your shares increase in value, the increase will only be taxed when you sell. And if you make a profit, the profit won't be taxed as ordinary income at rates as high as 39.6 percent; it'll receive more favorable capital gains treatment, with rates as low as 10 percent depending on the circumstances. But it *will* be taxed; with a Roth IRA, there'll be no tax if you meet the requirements.

The Fine Print

Just as with any deal that sounds great, there's some fine print to consider. For the Roth IRA to work best, you've got to know the rules. And you've got to follow them. Trip up and you'll trigger tax problems.

There's a lot to learn, in part because Roth IRAs are so new. The law that established Roth IRAs wasn't enacted until August 1997, and you weren't allowed to open a Roth IRA until January 1998. In addition, the Internal Revenue Service is still writing the regulations that will show, in detail, exactly how Roth IRAs will operate over the long haul. Nonetheless, the law provides the basic rules, enough to give you a good idea of what—and what *not*—to do.

As with a traditional IRA, for example, the most you can contribute to a Roth IRA is $2,000 for any given year. (Technically, the most you can contribute is either $2,000 or the total of your earned income, whichever is less.)

For married couples filing jointly, the maximum contribution overall is generally $4,000 (but no more than $2,000 per Roth IRA per spouse). If one spouse works and the other is at home, the maximum overall contribution is still $4,000 (but no more than $2,000 per account per spouse).

The Income Limits

The amount you can contribute each year to a Roth IRA is also limited by your income because Congress wanted to ensure that the Roth IRA appealed mainly to the middle class. Here are the limits:

- If you're single, you can make a full $2,000 contribution if your adjusted gross income for the year is less than $95,000. If you're married and filing jointly, you can make a full, combined contribution of $4,000 if your adjusted gross income is less than $150,000.
- If you're single, you can make only a partial contribution if your adjusted gross income is between $95,000 and $110,000. If you're married and filing jointly, you can make only a partial contribution if your adjusted gross income is between $150,000 and $160,000.
- If your adjusted gross income for the year is above these so-called phase-out limits, you can't contribute to a Roth IRA at all.
- Remember that these dollar limits are the *only* limits you use to figure whether you can contribute to a Roth IRA. In other words, it doesn't matter whether you are covered by a pension plan at work. (Pension plan coverage does matter if you're trying to figure out whether you can make a deductible contribution to a regular IRA.) As a result, if your adjusted gross income for a given year is less than the dollar limits shown here, you can contribute to a Roth IRA regardless of whether you are covered by a pension plan at work.

A Few More Rules

The most you can contribute to *all* IRAs is $2,000 a year if you're single or $4,000 overall if you're married and filing jointly. In other words, the government looks at all your IRAs—including Roth IRAs and traditional IRAs (deductible and nondeductible alike)—and applies a single annual contribution limit across the board.

What does that mean? If you're single, you can't contribute $2,000 to a traditional deductible IRA, $2,000 to a Roth IRA, and $2,000 to a traditional nondeductible IRA. The overall annual limit per person on IRA contributions is $2,000. Period. Education IRAs aren't counted toward this across-the-board limit, so you could contribute $2,000 to a Roth IRA plus another $500 to an education IRA if you like.

Some of the Roth IRA rules can work in your favor. For instance, you have until April 15 to contribute to a Roth IRA and have it count for the preceding tax year. (Just be sure to let your Roth IRA custodian or trustee know which year your contribution is for.)

And remember: You may contribute to a Roth IRA for any year in which you have earned income, or "taxable compensation," such as wages, salary, commissions, tips, bonuses, and so on. And don't forget that you may contribute to a Roth IRA no matter how old you are.

How to Qualify for Tax Benefits

Okay, what about all those juicy tax benefits you've heard so much about? They're available, but they come with a few strings attached.

In general, withdrawals from a Roth IRA are fully tax-free—no federal income tax and no penalty to pay. However, you generally escape the tax traps *only* if you meet two conditions: (1) If you withdraw money after your Roth account has been open at least five years *and* (2) the withdrawal occurs under *at least one* of these four circumstances:

1. You have reached age 59½.
2. Proceeds are paid to a beneficiary or your estate because of your death.
3. You've become disabled.
4. You use the money for expenses as a first-time homebuyer. (To find out how this rule works, see Figure 12.1.)

If your withdrawal meets these two conditions, the tax experts call it a "qualified distribution," and it'll escape federal taxation and penalty entirely.

Figure 12.1   First-Time Homebuyers

Withdrawals from Roth IRAs generally escape taxation and penalties if you use the money for expenses as a first-time homebuyer. Here's a summary of the rules governing first-time homebuyers:

- The maximum lifetime withdrawal is $10,000 of earnings.
- The money must be used within 120 days of withdrawal to buy, build, or rebuild the first principal residence for either you, your spouse, or any child, grandchild, or ancestor of yours or your spouse.
- If the 120-day rule can't be met because of delay in acquiring the residence, you may put the money back into your Roth IRA without any tax consequence.
- Expenses may include "reasonable" settlement, financing, or other closing costs.
- The house need not be the first you've ever owned. A taxpayer qualifies as a first-time homebuyer if either the taxpayer (or spouse) hasn't had an ownership interest in a principal residence during the two years before acquiring the "new" house.

Source: Congressional Conference Committee Report

How does the five-year rule work? Just count the years. If you open an account today, this year will be your Roth IRA's first tax year. As a result, you can start making withdrawals without tax or penalty on the first day of the sixth tax year (as long as you meet the other requirements, too: you're 59½ or older, the withdrawal is made because of your death or disability, or you use the money for first-time homebuying expenses).

Here's an example: If you contributed to a Roth IRA in 1998, the earliest you can withdraw all your money without tax or penalty is January 2003. (In this example, the account has been open for five tax years, starting with 1998, so the first day of the sixth tax year is in January 2003.)

Breaking the Rules Won't Break the Bank

What if you don't meet the two conditions specified above? Your withdrawal will be taxed. That's not necessarily painful because only the *earnings* portion of your withdrawal gets taxed, not your contributions.

Another twist here also works to your advantage. The IRS assumes that your withdrawal from a Roth IRA comes first from contributions, then from earnings. This is a great feature because it not only saves you taxes but also saves you paperwork too.

The IRS assumption is especially helpful when you consider what happens in certain similar situations. For instance, if you have a nondeductible IRA (or if you have a regular IRA that contains nondeductible contributions), you know that part of the money in your account is taxable and part of it isn't. (Your original contributions were made with after-tax dollars, so they won't be taxed when withdrawn; the earnings haven't been taxed, so they will be taxed when withdrawn.)

In the government's eye, however, each withdrawal from a nondeductible IRA includes original contributions as well as earnings. In other words, you can't just assume that the withdrawals come first from contributions, then from earnings. Thus, for each withdrawal you make from a nondeductible IRA, you'll have to pay some tax. And you have to figure out what part of each withdrawal is taxable and what isn't (unless your account's custodian or trustee does the work for you).

The same rule generally holds true with annuities. The government says each payment you get from a commercial annuity that you purchased from an insurance company generally includes a tax-free return of your original investment plus a taxable distribution of your earnings. And you typically have to get a pencil and paper to figure out which part of each annuity payment is taxable and which isn't (unless your annuity's issuer does the work for you).

Because Roth IRAs work differently, you'll have less paperwork, fewer calculations, and fewer hassles overall. Here's an example: Say you contribute $2,000 today to a Roth IRA. Two years from now the account has grown in value to about $2,500. If you withdraw $1,000 at that time, none of it gets taxed.

Why? Because the IRS figures you withdrew the money from your original contribution, not your earnings. (Remember: When it comes to Roth IRAs, contributions come out first, then earnings.) And because your original contribution in this example totaled $2,000 and you withdrew only $1,000, there's no tax.

A Benefit for Multiple Roth Accounts

Here's another neat twist: If you have several Roth accounts to which you made contributions and you make a withdrawal before you're supposed to, you lump together all your Roth IRAs to help you figure out what part of your withdrawal (if any) is going to get taxed.

Here's how this works. Suppose you contribute $2,000 this year to Roth IRA 1 and $2,000 next year to Roth IRA 2. A few years later, your first Roth IRA has grown in value to $2,200 and your second Roth IRA has grown in value to $2,100.

At that point, you close your first Roth IRA and withdraw all $2,200. What part is taxable? None of it because in doing your tax calculations, you lump together all the contributions to all your Roth IRAs. In this example, you made a total of $4,000 in contributions to all your Roth IRAs. The $4,000 of total contributions is greater than the $2,200 you withdrew. Therefore, none of the $2,200 withdrawal gets taxed because the government says that your Roth IRA withdrawals come first from contributions, then from earnings.

When Earnings Get Taxed

Okay, so what happens if you don't make a "qualified distribution"? In other words, what happens if you pull *all* the money out of your Roth IRA before you're supposed to—including all your original contributions plus all the money your account has earned? In that case, you'll have to report the earnings as income; the earnings will be subject to federal income tax and treated as ordinary income.

Will the earnings also face a 10 percent penalty? Not if an exception applies. And Congress was clear about this when it approved the legislation: "The same exceptions to the early withdrawal tax that apply to IRAs apply to [Roth IRAs]," according to a congressional conference report on Roth IRAs.

Escaping the Penalty

Congress's report means that the earnings from your Roth IRA withdrawal will not face the 10 percent penalty on premature withdrawals if the withdrawal is made under any of these circumstances:

- You're 59½ or older.
- You're disabled.
- You've died.
- The withdrawal is part of a series of substantially equal withdrawals made at least annually over your life expectancy or the life expectancy of you and your beneficiary.
- The money is for medical expenses for which you haven't been reimbursed and which exceed 7.5 percent of your adjusted gross income.
- The money pays for medical insurance premiums for you, your spouse, and your dependents, but only if you've lost your job.
- You use the money for "qualified higher education expenses" either for yourself, your spouse, or any child or grandchild of either yours or your spouse.
- You use the money for expenses as a first-time homebuyer.

(This is just a summary of how the exceptions work. For details, see Chapter 7 about the exceptions to penalties for withdrawals from a traditional IRA.)

As a general rule, you'll want to keep your money in a Roth IRA as long as possible. That way, you'll avoid all federal income tax on withdrawal, no matter how much you withdraw, and your money gets to grow inside your account year after year without being nibbled away by taxes.

In other words, you'll want to keep your money in your account for at least five years to ensure that all withdrawals escape federal taxation. Unfortunately, the law doesn't offer much detail on exactly how the five-year requirement is defined, so look for IRS guidance on this point.

In general, if you have only one Roth IRA, it's four years old, and you withdraw everything from your account, you'll have to include the account's earnings in your income and will be taxed on it. If your account is six years old in this example, the withdrawn earnings avoid tax and penalty altogether.

Recapping the Withdrawal Rules

The rules on withdrawals can get pretty confusing. So here's a brief recap:

- Money you contribute to a Roth IRA has already been taxed, so when you withdraw your contributions, they won't be taxed again.
- The only part of your Roth account that can be subject to taxation and penalty is the money your account earns for you over the years, whether it's in the form of interest, dividends, or price appreciation (on shares of stocks or shares of a mutual fund, for instance).
- For purposes of figuring any tax and/or penalty, remember that your withdrawals from a Roth IRA come first from contributions, then from earnings.
- If you keep your hands off your Roth IRA for at least five tax years, your earnings won't be taxed or penalized when you withdraw them as long as your withdrawals occur after you turn 59½ or are made as a result of your death, your disability, or are used for first-time home-buyer expenses.
- If you withdraw earnings, but don't meet the conditions listed above, your earnings may also be subject to a 10 percent penalty. But you can avoid this penalty if the withdrawals occur under any of the special penalty exceptions that apply to early withdrawals from regular, traditional IRAs. (The earnings that you withdraw from a Roth IRA won't be penalized, for example, if they're used to pay for certain college education costs; certain medical expenses; or medical insurance premiums if you're unemployed.)

Figure 12.2   Roth IRA versus a Taxable Account

Here's how a $2,000 deposit in a Roth IRA compares with a $2,000 deposit in a taxable account, such as a regular bank account, if each earns 5 percent a year for a lower-income taxpayer.

	After 5 Years	After 10 Years	After 15 Years	After 20 Years
Roth IRA	$2,553	$3,258	$4,158	$5,307
Taxable Account	2,463	3,032	3,734	4,598

Note: These numbers assume the investor is in the 15 percent federal tax bracket, and they ignore the impact of any state or local income tax, which would reduce the balances in the taxable account even further.

Is the Roth IRA for You?

Okay, so maybe now you have a pretty good idea of how Roth IRAs work and some basic understanding of the rules. The question is, should you choose a Roth IRA? It depends.

How Roth IRAs Compare with Taxable Accounts and Stocks

Roth IRAs versus taxable accounts.   If you face a choice between contributing to a Roth IRA or investing money in a regular taxable account, the Roth IRA generally wins because of its tax advantages.

Here's an example: Suppose you put $2,000 this year in a regular taxable account, such as a bank account, and you also put $2,000 into a Roth IRA. You leave the money alone for five years. Both accounts grow at 5 percent a year, as shown in Figure 12.2.

After five years, you'll have about $2,553 in the Roth account. But you'll have only about $2,463 in the taxable account. The Roth IRA leaves you with about $90 more. Why? Because the money your Roth IRA earns each year isn't taxed, but the money your regular bank account earns each year *is* taxed.

This example assumes you're in the 15 percent federal income tax bracket. If you're in a higher bracket, the difference will be even larger because taxes will take an even bigger bite out of the regular bank account's earnings each year.

Figure 12.3   Roth IRA versus Investment in Stock

If you invested $2,000 in a stock outright and also invested $2,000 in a Roth IRA that held stock, here's what you'd be left with when you cashed out (assuming an annual growth rate of 8 percent).

	After 5 Years	After 10 Years	After 20 Years
Roth IRA	$2,939	$4,318	$9,322
Taxable Account	$2,845	$4,086	$8,590

Note: These figures assume the investor is in the 15 percent federal tax bracket, so price appreciation in a taxable account is subject to a 10 percent federal capital gains tax treatment when the stock is sold. The figures ignore dividends, brokerage commissions, fees, and expenses on both accounts, as well as state and local income taxes on the taxable account.

Roth IRAs versus stocks.   Maybe a bank account isn't a fair example. Maybe you'd like to invest in something that could earn you more over time, such as stocks.

Suppose you put $2,000 this year in a stock and you contribute $2,000 to a Roth IRA. You leave the money alone for five years. Both investments grow at 8 percent a year.

After five years, both investments are worth $2,939, but if you cash in the stock at that time, you'll have only about $2,845 to put in your pocket. That's because you must pay a capital gains tax on the growth that's built up over the years. Even though capital gains tax rates are lower now than they were, you still have to pay some tax. The level of capital gains tax that you have to pay generally depends on your overall income tax rate.

Let's say you're in the 15 percent income tax bracket in this example; you'll probably have to pay a 10 percent capital gains tax. In this example, your $2,000 investment (consisting of after-tax dollars) grew to about $2,939, but the $939 in growth will be taxed at 10 percent so you'll have to fork over about $94 in capital gains tax, leaving you with a total of about $2,845, as seen in Figure 12.3.

With the Roth IRA, on the other hand, you'll have the full $2,939 to yourself. No federal tax is due. In this example, you're almost $100 ahead of the game. That's almost $100 more to put in your pocket. And the higher your tax bracket, the more you'll have to fork over in capital gains taxes for the taxable account, so the Roth IRA would look even better.

Roth IRAs versus Traditional IRAs

With traditional IRAs, you may be eligible for a big tax benefit up front. With Roth IRAs, the big tax advantage comes at the end. So do you want to eat your cake now or later?

It's no small matter. The same law that created Roth IRAs also expanded traditional IRAs so that many more taxpayers each year will be eligible for at least some tax deduction for their contributions.

With traditional IRAs, you must generally clear two hurdles to figure out whether you can claim a tax deduction for the amount you contribute. These hurdles (explained in detail in earlier chapters that focused on the traditional IRA) were introduced in 1986. They're not as strict as they once were, but they're still there.

One hurdle relates to your taking part in a pension or retirement plan at work. If you don't, you can make a fully deductible contribution to your IRA, no matter how much money you earn.

If you do take part in a pension or retirement plan at work, you still may be able to claim a deduction, but it generally depends on your overall level of income—another hurdle. These limits were fixed by the Tax Reform Act of 1986, and because they weren't indexed to rise with inflation each year, they remained frozen at the same level for ten years. As a result, fewer and fewer taxpayers each year were eligible for a deduction on their contributions to a traditional IRA.

The new law in 1997 changed that by allowing the limits to grow according to a set schedule through 2005 (for singles) and 2007 (for married couples filing jointly). As a result of the new law, more and more taxpayers will be able to claim at least some deduction for their contributions to traditional IRAs in the years ahead. This can mean big tax savings. If you're single and in the 15 percent income tax bracket, for instance, and you make a $2,000 fully deductible contribution to a traditional IRA, you save $300 in income tax.

Keep making deductible contributions to a traditional IRA year after year and the tax savings mount up, which is one reason traditional IRAs have become so attractive once again to many more Americans. It's also one reason why it'll be hard for some taxpayers to choose between a traditional IRA and a Roth IRA. (See Figure 12.4.)

Taking a Tax Break Now or Later

Another reason it's hard to choose between a traditional IRA and a Roth is that it isn't easy to pass up a tax break today for a tax break you may get in the future. Sure, Roth IRAs generally mean you'll be able to make tax-free withdrawals later on, but that may be a hard sell if you're eligible for a tax deduction today by contributing to a regular IRA.

Figure 12.4   Roth IRA versus Traditional IRA

Here's a handy at-a-glance look at how the Roth IRA compares with the traditional deductible IRA on some key points.

	Traditional IRA	Roth IRA
Earned income required	Yes	Yes
Maximum annual $2000 contribution	Yes	Yes
Contributions tax deductible	Yes	No
Earnings grow tax deferred	Yes	Yes
Withdrawals tax-free	No	Yes
Early withdrawal penalty	Yes	Yes
Exceptions to penalty	Yes	Yes
Mandatory withdrawals	Yes	No
Contributions after 70½ allowed	No	Yes
Avoids probate	Yes	Yes
Subject to federal estate tax	Yes	Yes
Beneficiary pays income tax	Yes	No
Rollovers from pensions	Yes	No
Rollovers from other IRAs	Yes	Yes

Note: The maximum annual contribution to either account is $2,000 or 100 percent of earned income. If you have a Roth and a traditional IRA, the maximum combined annual contribution is $2,000. Contributions to a traditional IRA are tax deductible, and withdrawals from a Roth IRA are tax-free under certain conditions. Withdrawals from either account may escape penalty if the rules are followed. Withdrawals from a traditional IRA are required after age 70½. A beneficiary who withdraws money from an inherited traditional IRA faces federal income tax. Rolling over a traditional IRA to a Roth IRA triggers federal income tax.
Source: Congressional Conference Committee

A Few Guidelines

With the Roth IRA, withdrawals are tax-free as long as you live by the rules. Which is better then—a Roth or a traditional IRA? There's no one-size-fits-all answer. But there are some general rules:

- If you qualify for a tax deduction from a traditional IRA and you expect to be in a lower tax bracket when you retire than when you contribute, the traditional deductible IRA is generally a better deal. (In other words, go for the tax deduction you can get from a regular IRA.)

- If you expect to be in the same federal income tax bracket when you withdraw money as you are when you contribute money, the traditional deductible IRA may be best.
- If you expect you'll need to tap your IRA to help pay for expenses in retirement, the regular IRA is generally a better choice.
- If you qualify for a deduction with a traditional IRA, you'll reduce your adjusted gross income. And because of the way tax rules work, if you can cut your adjusted gross income, you may be able to claim more itemized deductions. You may also be able to take greater advantage of the Hope Scholarship Credit and Lifetime Learning Credit as well as the tax credit you may be allowed for each child you have ($400 per child in 1998 and $500 per child in later years).
- If you expect to be in a higher tax bracket on retirement than you are when you contribute, the Roth IRA generally makes more sense.
- If you expect to withdraw money from your IRA in retirement and your financial circumstances are such that you'll be triggering a tax on your Social Security benefits, the Roth IRA may be a better choice.
- If you don't expect to need your IRA money in retirement and plan to use your IRA mainly as a way to build wealth and pass it along to the next generation (or to some other beneficiaries), the Roth IRA is the better choice.
- If you simply hate the idea of plowing through all the formulas and calculations that are triggered when you make minimum required withdrawals from a regular IRA, the Roth IRA wins easily.

Remember: These are only *general* rules. Whether they'll apply to your own financial circumstances depends on a lot of factors. It also depends on the assumptions you use in your calculations, so let's take a closer look at some of these points. (The calculations for some can be pretty involved and fairly complicated.)

If your tax bracket is lower in retirement.   The general rule is that traditional (deductible) IRAs are better than Roth IRAs if you expect to be in a lower federal tax bracket when you withdraw money (probably in retirement) than you are when you contribute. But trying to prove this can be tricky, depending on the numbers you use.

Say you're 30 years old. You're in the 28 percent federal tax bracket now but expect to be in the 15 percent bracket when you retire. Which deal is better for you: the Roth IRA or the traditional IRA? In general, the traditional IRA wins if you're eligible to claim the federal income tax deduction, as shown in Figure 12.5.

Figure 12.5   Roth IRA versus Traditional IRA

Here's how contributing to a Roth IRA may compare with contributing to a traditional deductible IRA, assuming you're in the 28 percent federal income tax bracket now but in the 15 percent bracket on retirement.

	Traditional IRA	**Roth IRA**
25-year-old	$827,149	$834,852
35-year-old	379,094	372,204
45-year-old	165,639	157,909
55-year-old	63,387	58,649

Note: These figures assume a $2,000 annual contribution to each account is made at the start of each year through age 70 and the accounts earn 8 percent a year. For a traditional IRA the money is assumed to be withdrawn in a lump sum at the end and (for convenience) the withdrawal taxed at 15 percent. The annual tax savings of $560 from contributions are assumed to be invested in a separate taxable account earning 8 percent a year (5.76 after accounting for federal tax). In most cases, a traditional IRA would generate a higher annual distribution over a 16-year payout period beginning at age 70.

If you invest $2,000 in a traditional IRA at the start of every year for 40 years, you'll wind up with $559,562.

If you invest $2,000 in a Roth IRA at the start of every year for 40 years, you'll also wind up with $559,562.

Both examples assume you earn 8 percent a year, and based on the numbers, you wind up in the same position: with $559,562. Where does the difference between Roth IRAs and regular IRAs come in?

One key difference shows up when you withdraw money. Withdrawals from regular IRAs are taxable; withdrawals from Roth IRAs generally aren't taxable. If, in our example, you invested in the regular (traditional) IRA and made a lump sum withdrawal from your account in retirement, you'd wind up with less than $559,562—probably far less because your entire withdrawal would be taxed as ordinary income.

If, however, you made a lump sum withdrawal from the Roth IRA, you'd wind up exactly the same as you were before—with $559,562—because the Roth IRA withdrawal would escape federal tax entirely.

Here it looks like the Roth IRA is the clear winner despite the general rule that says regular IRAs are better than Roth IRAs if you expect to be in a lower tax bracket in retirement. Well, just hold on a moment. Before you give the gold medal to the Roth IRA in this instance, let's do a little detective work first.

Is this example really fair to the regular IRA? No. Why? Because it gives credit to the Roth IRA's big tax benefit (which comes at the end on withdrawing money). But it doesn't give any credit to the regular IRA's big tax benefit (which comes at the beginning on contributing money).

Let's straighten things out and look at the numbers once again. You contribute $2,000 at the start of every year for 40 years to the Roth IRA. You wind up with $559,562. Let's say you also contribute $2,000 at the start of every year for 40 years to a regular IRA. You wind up with $559,562.

On withdrawing all your money from the Roth IRA, you still have $559,562 because withdrawals aren't taxed. But on withdrawing all your money from the regular IRA, you're left with about $476,000 because withdrawals from regular IRAs are taxed. (In fact, you'd probably be left with less depending on your tax bracket.)

Again it looks like the Roth IRA wins, but look more carefully. Each year that you contribute $2,000 to the regular IRA, *you also get an immediate income tax benefit of $560*. That's because you get to deduct $2,000 on your federal income tax return, and a $2,000 income tax deduction in the 28 percent federal bracket generates tax savings of $560 a year. Every year. *For 40 years* in this example.

So what happens to that money? If you don't spend the $560 each year and instead invest it in a separate account (earning 5.76 percent a year after taxes), you wind up with about $86,311 from that account alone.

The real answer to the problem: The Roth IRA leaves you with $559,562 even after the lump sum withdrawal; the regular IRA leaves you with about $476,000 after the lump sum withdrawal. Now add back in the $86,311 you got from your annual $560 in tax savings with the traditional deductible IRA. Suddenly, your regular IRA is worth about $562,000 *even after taxes*.

It turns out that, in this example, the regular IRA is really the winner. (This assumes, of course, that you qualified for the income tax deduction on the traditional IRA each year because your income was low enough. If you couldn't qualify, the Roth IRA would win easily.)

If you're in the same bracket before and after retirement.   Here's a look at what may happen if you expect to be in the same tax bracket in retirement as when you contribute. You're in the 31 percent federal income tax bracket, and you expect to be in the same bracket on retirement. You save $2,000 a year at the end of each year in a regular traditional IRA. The resulting federal income tax deduction saves you $620 a year.

You put the savings in a taxable account earning 10 percent a year (6.9 percent after accounting for the tax). At the end of five years, you withdraw all the money. Your regular IRA has $12,210, but after paying tax you net about $8,425. Add to that the amount you saved in your taxable account ($3,558) and you wind up with about $11,983.

Let's say you also save $2,000 a year at the end of each year in a Roth IRA. The account earns 10 percent a year. At the end of five years, your account is worth about $12,210. You withdraw the entire sum and still wind up with $12,210 because Roth IRA withdrawals aren't taxed if the rules are met. You've met the rules here. The Roth IRA wins.

Score: Roth IRA, $12,210; traditional IRA, $11,983.

Here the Roth wins even though the general rule says that traditional IRAs are better than Roth IRAs if you expect to be in the same tax bracket when you withdraw money as you are when you contribute. But the difference in this example isn't huge, and the result of the calculation could easily change if different assumptions are used or if you go about the calculation in a different way.

Suppose you're in the 28 percent income tax bracket and you expect to be in the same bracket when you retire. The amount you plan to save will earn 10 percent a year. Now let's see how the numbers work when a slightly different formula is used.

Let's say you make the full $2,000 contribution to a regular IRA at the end of each year for 20 years. Each net contribution consists of $1,440 of your own money and $560 in tax savings. In the end, you wind up with $114,550. You withdraw the money in a lump sum. After paying income tax on the withdrawal (at 28 percent, let's say), you net $82,476.

You also contribute $1,440 a year at the end of each year in after-tax dollars to a Roth IRA. (Remember: You may contribute only after-tax dollars to a Roth IRA, so for purposes of this example, $2,000 after taxes—at a rate of 28 percent—equals $1,440.) At the end of 20 years you wind up with $82,476.

In this example, the Roth IRA and the regular IRA turn out to have exactly the same result. Why? The tax benefits from both types of IRA are equal. Picture a seesaw: On one side is the front-loaded tax benefit of the regular IRA (the deduction you get on making contributions—assuming, of course, that you qualify), and on the other side is the back-loaded tax benefit of the Roth IRA (the tax-free withdrawals). In this example and with this formula, the two sides are perfectly in balance; there is no winner (except you, the saver!).

If you're in a higher tax bracket in retirement.   What if you're in a higher tax bracket when you retire than when you contribute? In this case, the Roth IRA appears to be a clear winner, with no fudging. Here's an example:

Let's say you're in the 28 percent income tax bracket during your working years. You decide to contribute $2,000 to a regular IRA at the end of each year for ten years. Your account earns 10 percent a year, and wind up with $31,875. You withdraw the entire amount in a lump sum and wind up with about $21,994 after paying tax at a rate of 31 percent.

Your annual contributions to the regular IRA allow you a tax deduction, generating tax savings of $560 a year that you invest in a taxable account earning 10 percent (or 7.2 percent after accounting for tax). This gives you a

Figure 12.6   Roth IRA versus Traditional IRA

Here's how contributing to a Roth IRA may compare with contributing to a traditional deductible IRA. The figures assume you're in the 28 percent income tax bracket now but will pay at a 30 percent bracket on retirement.

	Traditional IRA	**Roth IRA**
25-year-old	$670,653	$834,852
35-year-old	302,948	372,204
45-year-old	130,229	157,909
55-year-old	48,982	58,649

Note: The amounts assume a $2,000 annual contribution to each account is made at the start of each year through age 70 and the accounts earn 8 percent a year. For a traditional IRA the money is assumed to be withdrawn in a lump sum at the end and taxed at 30 percent; the annual tax savings of $300 from contributions are assumed to be invested in a separate taxable account earning 8 percent a year (6.8 percent after accounting for federal tax). In all cases, a Roth IRA would generate a higher annual distribution over a 16-year payout period beginning at age 70.

total of about $7,811. Add that to the amount you net from the regular IRA ($21,994) and you end up with a grand total of about $29,800.

You also contribute $2,000 at the end of each year for ten years to a Roth IRA, and at the end you've accumulated $31,875. You withdraw the entire amount in a lump sum and still wind up with $31,875 because Roth IRA withdrawals are tax-free if you meet the rules, and you've met the rules. The Roth account wins.

Score: Roth account, $31,875; regular IRA, $29,800.

Be Careful about Software

Yes, all this can get really complicated. And yes, it involves a lot of number crunching. That's why it may be best for you to consult an accountant or other tax or financial adviser who can run some numbers under different sets of variables using computer software. (For software you can get on your own, see "For More Information . . ." at the end of this chapter.)

No matter who runs the numbers, keep careful track of the assumptions the adviser uses. And if you don't understand something, it doesn't mean you're stupid. Just stop the process and ask a question.

Remember: The more complicated the calculation, the greater the opportunity for fudging. A sneaky financial adviser will always want to make things sound as complicated as possible to dazzle you with numbers and formulas and confuse you as much as possible—and make you appear as stupid as possible—so that he or she can supply the "real answers" and then make a sale. Watch out!

Some Final Points

- Withdrawal rules for beneficiaries of Roth IRAs are similar to the rules governing traditional IRAs. For example, if you inherit a Roth IRA from someone who is not your spouse, you generally must withdraw at least a minimum amount from the account each year based on your own life expectancy. This at least lets you stretch out the withdrawals, and remember that these withdrawals are tax-free. (You also have the option to simply withdraw all the money by Dec. 31 of the fifth year after the year of the original owner's death.) If you inherit a Roth IRA from your spouse, however, you generally may roll it over into your own Roth IRA. This means you won't have to make minimum withdrawals. (But you can always withdraw assets from the account if you wish.)
- Keep in mind the eligibility limits on who can and can't contribute to a Roth IRA. The amount you may contribute is phased out if you're single and your adjusted gross income is between $95,000 and $110,000, or if you're married filing a joint return and your adjusted gross income is between $150,000 and $160,000. But if you're close to any of these limits, you can take steps to get around them. For instance, if you're eligible for a year-end bonus or commission from your job, wait until the end of the year to see where your income for the year will stand. If possible, consider pushing off some compensation until the following tax year so you won't lose your eligibility for contributing to a Roth IRA. Here's another way to try to push yourself below the income limits: If you've got money invested in an account that generates taxable interest (such as a regular bank account, corporate bonds, or a taxable money market account or taxable money market mutual fund), think about cashing out and switching the money to a tax-free investment (such as a tax-exempt money market fund, municipal bonds, or a municipal bond mutual fund) or a tax-deferred investment (such as Series EE U.S. savings bonds). If you've got a 401(k) or 403(b) plan or similar arrangement at work that lets you contribute salary or wages, fund it to the maximum if you can afford it so as to reduce your overall income and move you below the Roth IRA income limits.

- To avoid taxes on your Roth account, it's best to simply keep your money in your Roth IRA for at least five years. But keep in mind that you may not have to tie up your money quite so long. "The five-year holding period begins with the taxable year to which the contribution relates, rather than the year in which the contribution is actually made," according to a congressional conference committee report. If you contribute $2,000 to a Roth IRA in April 1999 but tell your IRA trustee or custodian that the contribution is for the 1998 tax year, then the five-year clock starts ticking in 1998, not 1999. As a result, the earliest you can withdraw money without tax or penalty in this example is *still* 2003 even though you made your first contribution in 1999. (The reason: the first contribution in this example was attributed to the 1998 tax year even though you actually made it in 1999.) As this example shows, the actual holding period can be somewhat less than five full years.
- To ensure you're eligible for all the benefits of a Roth IRA, make sure you designate your account as a Roth IRA when you open it. There are several different types of IRAs out there. If you want a Roth IRA, make sure your IRA trustee or custodian knows you're opening a Roth IRA. (You can probably get this done easily by checking the appropriate box or completing the right section on your account application.)

To Sum Up . . .

Here's a quick summary of the potential advantages and disadvantages of contributing to a Roth IRA:

Advantages

- Earnings in your account aren't taxed each year. Tax is deferred, or avoided entirely, depending on when and for what purpose you make withdrawals.
- In general, you may be able to contribute up to $2,000 a year, and if you're married your spouse may also be able to contribute up to $2,000 a year.
- Your withdrawals may escape tax altogether if you abide by the rules. In general, withdrawals are entirely tax-free if your account has been open at least five years *and* your withdrawal occurs after you reach 59½ or because of your disability or death or if the money is used for expenses under the first-time homebuyer rule.
- You aren't required to withdraw money from a Roth IRA ever, even after you turn 70½.

- You may contribute to a Roth IRA at any time as long as you have earned income (taxable compensation) even after you turn 70½.
- If you die and your beneficiary inherits your IRA, your beneficiary won't have to pay income tax for money withdrawn from the account.
- You may generally roll over, or transfer, money from one Roth IRA to another Roth IRA without tax consequence.

Disadvantages

- You don't get a federal income tax deduction for money you contribute to a Roth IRA.
- The maximum annual contribution is $2,000 or 100 percent of your earned income, whichever is less. And the overall maximum annual contribution to all IRAs (including regular IRAs and Roth IRAs) is $2,000.
- If your adjusted gross income is high enough, you may be able to make only limited contributions to a Roth IRA or no contributions at all.
- If you withdraw all your money before your Roth account has been open five years, earnings may be subject to federal income tax (and treated as ordinary income) plus a 10 percent penalty.
- The earnings portion of your withdrawals could be subject to state and/or local income tax depending on where you live.

For More Information . . .

- T. Rowe Price Associates, a Baltimore mutual fund company, has a newsletter devoted almost entirely to the new rules for IRAs. *Special Report: The New Tax Legislation* also offers a detailed comparison of the Roth IRA versus the traditional deductible IRA. For your free copy, write: T. Rowe Price, 100 East Pratt St., Baltimore, MD 21202, or call 1-800-225-5132. The newsletter includes worksheets you can use to figure out which option is best.
- T. Rowe Price also sells a software program for $9.95, the T. Rowe Price IRA Analyzer, that helps you make comparisons. To order the software, call 1-800-332-6407. For more information, contact the company's Web site at www.troweprice.com.
- Ernst & Young, the worldwide accounting and financial consulting firm, has a Web site that includes a software program you can download to calculate how contributions to a Roth IRA compare with contributions to a traditional deductible and nondeductible IRA. Contact this Web site: www.ey.com/pfc.

- Merrill Lynch brokerage has a booklet about the 1997 tax act that includes information about the Roth IRA and offers some investment strategies. For a free copy, call 1-800-MERRILL, or contact the company's Web site at www.ml.com.
- While you're on the Internet, keep in mind that lots of other mutual fund companies, brokerages, and other organizations have tons of information about the Roth IRA, and some have programs you can use online to help you figure out whether a Roth IRA or a traditional IRA is best for you. For the Fidelity funds site: www.fidelity.com. For the Vanguard funds site: www.vanguard.com. For the Strong funds site: www.strong-funds.com. A software company also has a site to keep you informed about Roth IRAs: www.rothira.com.

Converting to a Roth IRA

Converting a regular IRA to a Roth IRA lets you cash in on all the benefits of Roth accounts, but you'll have to pay a big tax when you convert. Is it worth the money? This chapter examines the special one-time tax treatment you'll receive if you convert to a Roth IRA and sizes up the benefits and drawbacks of conversions.

The benefits of converting a traditional IRA to a new Roth IRA are tremendous. No doubt about it.

That's why you've heard so much talk about cashing out of a traditional IRA and putting the money into a Roth IRA. There's been a ton of publicity and loads of advertisements. You're bound to see more too. Why? Converting is great. The Roth IRA gives you lots of flexibility, lots of tax benefits, and a neat way to pass IRA dollars to the next generation if you want.

To get all these benefits, however, you've got to pay first. And you may wind up paying through the nose. Congress isn't stupid. When the government passed a batch of new tax laws in 1997, some were intended to cut taxes, some were aimed at boosting tax revenues, and others were designed to do both.

Keep that in mind if you're thinking about converting a traditional IRA to a Roth IRA. Sure, it could save you money—a lot of it—in the long run, but it'll also cost you in taxes up front. So take a moment to think of that, and think carefully. Do you want to pay taxes now or later?

Tempting Tax Breaks

For many investors, paying taxes now or later is a crucial question. The long-range tax savings you can get from converting to a Roth IRA are mighty tempting. However, not only are they down the road, but to get them, you've got to pay some taxes.

You don't have to be a math whiz to figure it out. The higher the amount you convert, the more you'll pay in taxes. And the higher your marginal federal income tax bracket, the more you'll pay because for every dollar that you convert, you're going to have to pay some tax. If you convert a traditional deductible IRA, every dollar will be taxed. If you convert a traditional nondeductible IRA, the earnings will be taxed.

Sure, you can use some of the money you convert to pay the tax bill, but that doesn't make sense. Odds are you won't have enough years in your lifetime to make up for the money you lose by tapping your existing IRA to pay the tax. Even some of the most vocal advocates of converting acknowledge this point, so the best way in the long run to make a conversion work is to pay the tax bill up front, out of pocket. In fact, it's really the *only* way that a conversion makes sense. You've got to pay the tax out of your own pocket; you've got to write a check to the IRS.

How painful can that be? If you're in the 15 percent federal bracket and you convert a $10,000 traditional IRA to a Roth IRA, you'll have to pay $1,500 in federal income tax. In the 28 percent bracket you'll pay $2,800; in the 36 percent bracket, it's $3,600.

Maybe that's no problem for you. Maybe that's just loose change, burning a hole in your pocket. But what if you're talking about bigger numbers? Say you convert a $50,000 traditional IRA to a Roth IRA. In the 28 percent bracket, you'll pay $14,000 in federal tax. Up front. Out of pocket. In the 36 percent bracket, you'll have to fork over $18,000. Do you have that much money just hanging around? If so, do you feel like parting with it? And handing it over to the IRS?

And that's just federal income tax. If you live in a state that levies its own income tax, your final tax bill will probably be more, maybe much more, depending on your state's rules.

Sure, you won't have to pay a penalty. If you convert a traditional IRA to a Roth IRA, you won't have to face the additional 10 percent penalty on early withdrawals even if you're under age 59½. And for some people, at least, affordability may still not be an issue, no matter how high the tax bill is.

A Tax Is Still a Tax

Still, some people just hate the idea of paying a tax to the government. It's against their principles. Even though it could save them money in the long run, they'll refuse to budge—and that's why Roth conversions may prove to be a harder sell than proponents are willing to admit.

Suppose you're an accountant, financial planner, or other type of professional adviser. Your client drops by to ask about converting his traditional IRA to a Roth IRA. He's Rich Mr. Pennybags, and he's got $100,000 salted away, money he's been saving for years toward his retirement. He's really excited. He wants to convert. You tell him about the benefits. He's more excited. You tell him it makes sense. You spin your computer screen around and show him exactly how the numbers work and how they can work for him. He's practically ecstatic. "Sounds great!" he says. "What do I have to do?"

"Well, you've got to pay some taxes," you say.

"How much?" says he.

You pull out your calculator and crunch some quick numbers. Or maybe you even run the numbers through his tax return on your computer screen. Finally, the key number pops up: he'll have to hand over $31,000 in federal income taxes. And, oh, yes, there's a state income tax bill too. Maybe as much as $10,000. And suddenly your client isn't smiling anymore. In fact, he's downright angry.

"Well," you say, "you'll have to pay it eventually. When you take money out of your traditional IRA, you'll have to pay taxes then." But your client won't bite. "I'll pay what I owe when the time comes," he declares. "But I'm not paying one cent now." He leaves your office in a huff.

Don't laugh. That scene could be played out repeatedly throughout the country when people start to understand the details, the costly implications of converting to a Roth IRA. So before you think about converting, before you even consider whether you can afford it, think about whether you want to do it and how you'll feel afterward. What does your gut tell you?

If you decide to move ahead anyway, the future may not be so bleak. Yes, there's a tax due. And yes, it's smarter to pay out of pocket. But there are some things you can do to soften the blow a bit.

How to Convert

First, the basics. If you've got a traditional IRA, you *can* roll over the money into a Roth IRA. There's no limit on the amount you can convert, and it doesn't get counted against the $2,000 annual limit on contributions. Thus, you can roll over money from a regular IRA to a Roth IRA in a given year if you qualify, and you may also contribute $2,000 to a Roth IRA in the same year if you qualify.

In many cases, you can convert to a Roth IRA simply by notifying your bank, brokerage, or mutual fund company and filling out some forms. In other words, you don't actually have to move the money from one institution to another or from one fund to another; you can simply designate your existing IRA as a Roth IRA. (For details and forms, contact the institution that's holding your IRA—that is, the custodian or trustee. You may have already received a mailing from your financial institution or mutual fund company showing the details of the potential benefits and costs of converting.)

Cashing in on the Benefits

Once you convert, your traditional IRA becomes a Roth IRA, and you do, indeed, get all the associated benefits just as you would if you had simply contributed the annual $2,000 to a Roth.

In other words, if your money is in the Roth account long enough and if your withdrawals meet the rules, the money comes out tax-free. No tax. None at all.

What if you don't want to make any withdrawals? You just want to sit on your money as long as possible? That's okay too. There's no requirement to begin making withdrawals by age 70½ as there is with a traditional IRA. No minimum distributions. No need to check the life expectancy tables. No need to decide whether to recalculate each year. Just sit tight and let your money keep growing inside your account *tax-free.*

A Break for Beneficiaries

What happens to the account when you die? Yes, it'll be included as part of your taxable estate for purposes of figuring whether any federal estate tax is due. But the money gets passed to your beneficiary, directly and automatically, thus bypassing the probate process just as it would with a traditional IRA. Unlike the traditional IRA, however, your beneficiary won't have to pay income tax on the withdrawals. So yes, the Roth IRA is sweet. Very sweet.

Limits on Roth Conversions

As you might expect, there are limits. For example, you may convert a traditional IRA to a Roth IRA only if your adjusted gross income isn't more than $100,000 for the year in which you convert.

Here again, the government's aim is to make Roth IRAs and other IRAs work mainly for the middle class. And conversions are available only if you're single or married and filing jointly; you're not eligible if you're married but filing separately.

If your income is close to the limit, you do get a bit of a break. To see if you're eligible to convert, you figure your adjusted gross income *before* taking into account the money you plan to convert.

What does that mean? Say your adjusted gross income is $90,000 for the year, and you'd like to convert a $20,000 traditional IRA to a Roth IRA in that year. To figure out whether you'd be eligible for a conversion, your adjusted gross income in this example would be $90,000, not $110,000. In other words, strictly for this eligibility test don't include the amount you plan to convert; just figure your adjusted gross income as you normally would.

When You're Close to the Limit

If you're close to the $100,000 dollar limit and you want to be sure you don't exceed it, think about the same sort of steps outlined in Chapter 12 for keeping below the eligibility limit when making annual Roth IRA contributions.

For instance, wait until the end of the year to see how much in earnings you'll have. After all, you may not be paid in a steady weekly or monthly salary; you may be eligible for year-end bonuses or commissions, and these count toward figuring your adjusted gross income. If you're close to the $100,000 limit and your year-end bonus or commission might push you over the top, see if you can defer some income into the next tax year so that you'll be eligible to convert in the current year.

If you have investments that generate taxable income, think about cashing them in and putting the money instead into investments that generate tax-exempt interest, such as tax-free money market mutual funds, or investments that generate tax-deferred interest, such as Series EE U.S. savings bonds. That's the good news.

By now you know the bad news. If you convert, the money you transfer from your traditional IRA to a Roth IRA (or the money in your traditional IRA that you've now designated as a Roth IRA) will be taxed as ordinary income. In other words, the IRS will view it as a taxable distribution even if you don't actually withdraw and spend the money, even if the money never touches your hands. And you'll have to pay federal income tax on it according to your tax bracket, as described earlier. In fact, depending on the size of the amount you convert, you could be pushed into a higher tax bracket.

A Big Break for 1998

The picture isn't entirely bleak, however. If you convert in 1998, the IRS won't view the conversion as a single lump sum addition to your income. Instead, you can treat it as if it had been converted in equal installments over four years (starting with the tax year in which the conversion occurred).

What does that mean? Say you decide to convert a $100,000 traditional IRA to a Roth IRA in 1998. Normally, you'd have to report the entire $100,000 as income for the year, which could easily lift you into a much higher tax bracket than usual, and you'd be hammered by the resulting federal tax bill (not to mention any additional state tax that may be due).

Because you make the conversion in 1998, however, you can treat it, for tax purposes, as if you had converted $25,000 in 1998, $25,000 in 1999, $25,000 in 2000, and $25,000 in 2001. With this method, at least the tax tab won't be as great as it otherwise would be.

Converting a nondeductible IRA.   Don't forget that these tax rules also apply if you convert a traditional *nondeductible* IRA to a Roth IRA. (And converting a nondeductible IRA to a Roth IRA is really a great idea.) Remember that with a traditional nondeductible IRA, only the earnings will be subject to tax, not the original contributions (which you made with your after-tax dollars). Normally, you'd have to include all the earnings as income for the tax year, but for 1998 only you'll qualify for the special tax treatment, allowing you to treat the conversion as if you had received the taxable earnings over four years instead of just one.

If you convert a traditional IRA that holds some nondeductible contributions, you must figure out what part will be taxed on conversion. You can't try to avoid tax by "cherry-picking" your traditional IRS and converting only your nondeductible contributions. The IRS says that at least some of the amount you convert will be taxed, so you must do the calculation first. This rule also applies if you own more than one traditional IRA, at least one of which includes nondeductible contributions, and you plan to convert some of your traditional IRA dollars. In general, the calculation is the same you'd use when simply withdrawing money from a traditional IRA that includes nondeductible contributions. (For details, see Chapter 10.)

Here's an example that shows how the rule applies to a Roth conversion: Jason has three traditional IRAs totaling $333,000, including $6,000 in nondeductible contributions. He wants to convert $100,000 from his traditional IRAs to a Roth IRA. To figure out how much will be taxed, he divides the amount of nondeductible contributions ($6,000) by the total value of his IRAs ($333,000) and states the result as a percentage. In this example, his nondeductible contributions account for 1.8 percent of the total value of his traditional IRAs. As a result, 1.8 percent of the conversion amount *will not* be taxed; the remainder *will* be taxed. In this instance, $1,800 of the conversion amount will escape federal tax, but the remaining $98,200 of the conversion amount will be subject to federal income tax.

This special tax treatment applies *only* to conversions that are made by December 31, 1998. If you convert in later years, you'll have to report as income the entire amount you convert from a traditional deductible IRA and the entire earnings from a nondeductible IRA in the year you convert.

No penalty for converting.   No matter what year you convert, you won't be subject to the traditional IRA's 10 percent premature withdrawal penalty, even if you're under 59½.

You may also be eligible for some unrelated federal tax breaks that could ease the tax burden you'd otherwise face by converting.

Other tax breaks.   If you have children, for example, you may be able to claim a credit against your federal tax for each child in your household. Congress set the credit at $400 per child for the 1998 tax year and boosted it to $500 per child for 1999 and later years. Whether you're able to claim the credit generally depends on your income.

Look at it this way: The credit didn't exist before and now it does. If you can claim it, you can consider it "free" money from the federal government, money you weren't entitled to before. Why not consider it simply as an offset to the higher federal tax bill you'll incur by converting a traditional IRA to a Roth IRA?

Education credits can help.   The same holds true for two education-related credits that also took effect for 1998 and later years, the Hope Scholarship Credit and the Lifetime Learning Credit. If you or someone in your household is eligible for these credits (which generally can be used for college education expenses), these, too, may be used as a kind of offset against the tax you must pay for converting to a Roth IRA. (The Hope Scholarship Credit is generally limited to $1,500 per student per year for the first two years of college education; the Lifetime Learning Credit is generally limited to $1,000 a year through 2001 and $2,000 a year thereafter.)

The 1997 tax law also contained some other tax benefits, mainly deductions rather than credits, which you could also look at as "found money," a way to reduce the tax burden you face by converting.

Options When Switching from Your Classic IRA

You also get a few options for making the conversion from a traditional IRA to a Roth. You can simply rechristen your traditional IRA as a Roth IRA, as outlined earlier. In addition, you can transfer the money directly from one custodian to another (from a bank to a brokerage, for example). Or you can roll over the money from one institution to another or from one account to another.

Just remember that if you choose the rollover, you've got to complete the move within 60 days, as you would when rolling over money from one traditional IRA to another.

Free Transfers

Here's another point to keep in mind: You can freely transfer money from one Roth IRA to another Roth IRA without tax consequence. And, blessedly, you're not limited based on your income, so there's no complicated formula to figure out. If you're using a mutual fund to hold your Roth IRA and you want to transfer the money to another fund in the same family, you can do it (subject to your fund family's requirements). Likewise, you can take money out of a Roth IRA at one financial institution and move it to another financial institution without triggering tax consequences.

When the Clock Starts to Tick

As outlined in the previous chapter, withdrawals from Roth IRAs generally escape taxation if the money you withdraw has been in the account for at least five tax years. If you convert a traditional IRA to a Roth IRA, the five-year clock starts ticking in the tax year in which the conversion was made.

If your account has been open at least five years, your withdrawals come out free of federal income tax and free of penalty but only if the withdrawals are made under *any* of these conditions:

- You've reached age 59½.
- You're disabled.
- The money is withdrawn as a result of your death.
- You use the money to buy your first home.

Avoiding Tax and Penalty

Meet one of the these conditions and your withdrawals are absolutely free of federal tax and penalty. And, as outlined earlier, you don't have to withdraw any money at any time if you don't want to; it can continue to grow, tax-free, as long as you want.

If your withdrawals don't meet one of the conditions, any earnings on which you haven't already paid tax will be treated as income and will be subject to federal income tax. But keep in mind that, under the Roth rules, your withdrawals will be treated as coming from contributions first, not earnings. So until the amount you withdraw exceeds the entire amount you contributed, you're all set—no tax.

If you do wind up withdrawing earnings without meeting any of the conditions listed above, the earnings may also be subject to a 10 percent federal penalty for early withdrawal, and that's on top of any federal income tax you have to pay.

Even Earnings May Escape Penalty

Even with earnings, some breaks are available if you withdraw early. For instance, the earnings generally won't be subject to penalty if the withdrawal is made under *any* of these circumstances:

- You're 59½ or older.
- Withdrawals are made because of your disability.
- Withdrawals are made because of your death (so payments to beneficiaries or to your estate won't face the penalty).
- The withdrawal is part of a series of substantially equal payments made at least annually over your life expectancy, or the life expectancy of you and your beneficiary.
- The money is used to pay unreimbursed medical expenses that exceed 7.5 percent of your adjusted gross income.
- The money pays for health insurance premiums if you've lost your job.
- You use the money for expenses under the first-time homebuyer rule.
- You use the money to pay for certain college education expenses.

But let's face it: If you've gone this far—if you've made the conversion and paid the up-front tax—odds are you didn't make the move simply to start withdrawals.

Chances are that you fully understand the benefits of a Roth IRA and you plan to keep the money in the account for a long time, perhaps as long as you're alive.

Should You Convert?

Does a conversion make sense for you? Well, it depends.
Here are some general guidelines:

- Converting may make a lot of sense if your regular IRA has been open for only a short time and most of the money in the account is from nondeductible contributions. In this case, most of the money you convert won't be subject to tax at all because it has already been taxed. Although the earnings will be taxed, they won't also be subject to penalty on conversion because conversions escape the penalty. And besides, there won't be a lot of earnings to convert anyway.
- If you have a choice between converting a nondeductible IRA and a deductible IRA, convert the nondeductible IRA first for the reasons listed above.

- If you don't expect to need money from your IRA in retirement because you plan to have enough coming in from other sources, such as pensions, investments and Social Security, convert your regular IRA to a Roth IRA. If you're in this situation, you obviously want to pass as much money as possible to the next generation (or to other beneficiaries), and the Roth IRA is clearly a better way to do this than a regular IRA because you don't have to make minimum withdrawals from a Roth IRA while you're alive and your beneficiaries won't have to pay income tax on the withdrawals after they inherit your Roth account.
- Converting may make sense if you expect to be in a higher federal income tax bracket in retirement. If you're in a higher bracket in retirement and you withdraw money from a regular IRA, it'll be taxed heavily—as ordinary income—and it'll be taxed at a higher rate than the rate that applied when you made your original deductible contributions. (Roth withdrawals generally aren't taxable.)
- Remember that converting generally makes sense *only* if you have money from other sources to pay the tax bill due on conversion. If you have to use IRA money to pay the tax bill, you'll dig yourself a deep hole, and it's unlikely your Roth account will have enough years of growth to dig you out of the hole and put you ahead. If you use money from your regular IRA to pay the tax bill, you'll face a 10 percent penalty on that money. If you use money from your Roth IRA to pay the tax bill, it too will probably be subject to a penalty. (Some months after legislation was enacted that created the Roth IRA, Congress began debate on a measure that would impose a 20 percent penalty on IRA distributions that are used to pay the tax bill that's due for conversions.)
- Don't convert if you expect to have to make withdrawals from your Roth account later that won't qualify for tax-free and penalty-free treatment. In other words, don't convert if you plan to withdraw money before your account has been open five years or if your withdrawals won't meet the other conditions for favorable tax treatment (these conditions generally require that you be over 59½, the money comes out because of your death or disability, or you use it to pay for first-time homebuyer expenses). If you make withdrawals that don't qualify for favorable tax treatment, you'll suffer twice: your money won't be able to continue to grow in your Roth account to make up for the tax you had to pay on converting, and you'll have to pay a tax (and possibly a penalty) for the withdrawals you make in this example.
- Don't convert if you expect to be in a sharply lower federal income tax bracket when you retire. If you're in a lower bracket in retirement and you withdraw money from a regular IRA, it'll be taxed relatively lightly. But if you convert that IRA when you're in a high bracket, it'll be taxed heavily.

- Don't convert if you have only a little while until you retire *and* you expect to have to make withdrawals to make ends meet. If you convert in this case, you'll have to pay tax, but your money won't have enough time to grow to make up for the tax you had to shell out in the first place.
- Look closely at exactly how much you plan to convert. You don't have to convert all the money that's in your traditional IRA; you can convert only part if you wish. If you convert a big amount, this could push you into a much higher federal income tax bracket—especially if you do the conversion in 1999 or later, because then the entire amount of the conversion will have to be lumped in with the rest of your income for a single tax year. By converting in 1998, you spread the amount you convert into four different tax years, lessening the tax impact.
- If you're collecting Social Security benefits and you're thinking about converting, look carefully at the tax impact—not only on your overall income but also on your Social Security benefits. Social Security benefits generally aren't taxed, but they are if your income is high enough. If you convert, you'll have to include the amount of your conversion in your income, and this could be enough to trigger a tax on your Social Security. If your Social Security benefits are already subject to tax because of your overall income level, converting could cause a greater portion of your Social Security benefits to be taxed.

A Closer Look at the Scale: Time, Amount, and Growth

Let's take a closer look at some of the guidelines. For instance, one key factor obviously is *time*. In general, the more time you have, the more sense a conversion makes because the more time your account will be able to grow, *tax-free*, and help make up for the money you had to shell out to pay the tax bill for converting in the first place.

Right away you know that converting generally doesn't make sense if you've only a few years left until retirement and you expect you'll need the money to help meet expenses in retirement. Even in this case, though, converting may still make some sense depending on how much money you have to convert and how long you can afford to postpone withdrawals.

Say you're 55 years old and planning to retire in another seven years, at age 62. According to the government's life expectancy tables, you may have about 29 years remaining. Now suppose you don't need the money in retirement—your financial picture is all squared away, you're healthy, you come from a long line of people who tend to outlive the government's official life expectancy tables, and you'd like to pass all the money in your traditional IRA to the next generation.

In this case, converting may make sense because you may have plenty of time—perhaps as much as three decades or more—for your Roth IRA to earn enough, free of tax, to make up for the cash you had to fork over to pay the tax bill associated with converting.

If you're young and you have plenty of years left before retirement, converting may make the most sense because your Roth account will have many years of growth to overcome the hole you have to dig to pay the conversion tax.

Another key factor to bear in mind is the *amount* you plan to convert. In general, the bigger the sum, the greater your initial tax bill for converting and therefore the longer your Roth dollars will have to work to overcome this initial handicap.

This principle also works in reverse. In general, the smaller the sum you plan to convert, the smaller your initial tax levy for converting and the less your Roth account will have to work to overcome the handicap.

Time and amount aren't the only factors. *Growth* is another key variable. In general, the more your Roth account can grow, the more that converting makes sense, because the quicker you'll be able to compensate for your original conversion tax bill.

For this reason it seems to make sense to invest your Roth IRA dollars in a place that'll offer the greatest chance at the highest possible return. Chances are you'll want to avoid sticking your Roth IRA in a slow-growing bank account or investing your money in short-term U.S. Treasury securities or short-term government or corporate bond funds.

Instead, you'll want to stick your Roth money in stocks or in stock mutual funds, which historically have provided investors the greatest returns over the long haul. Yes, your account will fluctuate in value, because stocks—and stock mutual funds—tend to be the most volatile investments. But if you can stomach the roller-coaster ride and if you can invest for the very long haul— say 10 years or more—stocks and stock mutual funds may be the way to go.

You don't necessarily have to be an expert at picking the right stocks or the right stock funds; you can simply plop your Roth IRA dollars in a mutual fund whose performance is tied directly to one of the well-known stock market indexes, such as the Dow Jones Industrial Average of 30 blue chip stocks or the Standard & Poor's index of 500 large-company stocks.

What Money Will You Use?

Another key issue is where, exactly, you'll find the funds to pay the tax due on conversion. If you use money in a bank account or in short-term cashlike investments, such as money market mutual funds or three-month or six-month U.S. Treasury bills, for instance, you won't trigger much of a tax consequence. In fact, there may be no tax consequence at all. And using this type of asset may make some sense (if you can afford it) because these assets typically generate ordinary income, which is taxed at potentially high rates.

What if you plan to cash in some shares of stock or of stock mutual funds? First, you've got to consider the tax impact. Sure, the federal capital gains tax rates are lower now, but how long have you held the asset?

If you're going to cash in stock that you've held for decades, you may have a huge built-in capital gain. So if you sell now to pay your conversion tax, you may have to fork over some big bucks in federal capital gains tax first, despite the lower capital gains rates.

What Tax Will You Face?

Yes, you must pay a federal income tax upon converting, and your state or locality may levy a tax too. This is certainly a consideration, as outlined before. But what about when you retire? Will you be in a lower income tax bracket than you are when you convert?

In general, a lower bracket in retirement tends to favor the traditional IRA in your calculations because your withdrawals won't be taxed as much, leaving more in your account to keep growing tax-deferred. Of course it's true that Roth withdrawals will be entirely tax-free if you meet the rules, but a lower tax rate in retirement will tend to narrow the difference between a regular IRA and a Roth IRA.

Putting It All Together

Your decision whether to convert to a Roth IRA or keep your money in a traditional IRA hinges on a lot of variables. So it's hard to offer general rules because too many different factors are involved, but let's consider an example.

Converting a $25,000 traditional deductible IRA to a Roth IRA may make sense for 45-year-old Bill, according to Figure 13.1. Here, the Roth IRA delivers $33,071 more in retirement income. If he converts, he must pay a total of $7,900 in state and federal tax. He doesn't pay the tax out of the money he converts; he uses other sources to pay the bill, so he's able to put the full conversion amount into the Roth. To make for a valid comparison, then, we credit the regular IRA with an additional $7,900, which is put in a tax savings account. The regular IRA is worth $116,524 at retirement, and the tax savings account is worth $21,205, for a total of $137,729.

Bill then starts to withdraw money over a 20-year period. The money that remains in the accounts after each withdrawal continues to grow, but Bill must pay tax on each withdrawal from his regular IRA. Over the 20 years, he's able to withdraw a total of $172,518 from his regular IRA and the tax savings account.

Figure 13.1   Converting a Regular IRA to a Roth IRA

	Pretax Value at Retirement		Total After-Tax Withdrawals in Retirement		Net Gain
	Current IRA	Roth IRA	Current IRA	Roth IRA	
	$116,524	$116,524	$140,623	$205,589	
Tax savings account:	21,205	NA	31,894	NA	
Total value:	137,729	116,524	172,518	205,589	$33,071

Note: The numbers assume an 8 percent annual rate of return before retirement and a 7 percent annual rate of return after retirement; the investor retires at age 65 and withdraws over a 20-year period; and a federal tax rate of 28 percent before and after retirement plus a state rate of 5 percent for a combined effective rate of 31.6 percent. The "Tax Savings Account" assumes taxes that would have been paid in the IRA conversion are instead invested in a separate taxable account, which grows at the same rates as above. The value of this separate account is added to the "Current IRA" to make a valid comparison with the "Roth IRA," because the illustration assumes no money was taken out of the "Current IRA" to pay taxes due on conversion to a "Roth IRA."

Source: *The T. Rowe Price Report,* published by T. Rowe Price Associates.

If Bill converts to a Roth, his Roth is worth $116,524 at retirement. He then begins withdrawing from the Roth over 20 years. In total he's able to withdraw $205,589, which is more than the combined withdrawals from his regular IRA and his tax savings account. The Roth IRA's big advantage is that withdrawals aren't taxed. (See Figure 13.1.)

About the only way you can tell for sure whether converting all—or even a portion—of your traditional IRA makes sense for you is to use a computer. A computer program can help account for all the variables in your personal financial circumstances, and, fortunately, a lot of such programs are available. Some are do-it-yourself programs available from big mutual fund companies. You can buy one, or find one online. (For details, see "For More Information . . ." at the end of the chapter.)

It also makes sense to consult an accountant, financial planner, stock broker, or other financial adviser. Odds are such experts have their own programs and can also offer you advice on whether to convert. They may also be able to point out some factors you might otherwise overlook. (And there are many, many factors to consider when deciding about whether to convert.)

To Sum Up . . .

Just remember that if you can afford to pay the initial tax bill up front and out-of-pocket, the Roth IRA has a lot of attractive features waiting for you.

With a Roth IRA, the earnings inside your account grow tax-free, and in the end you get to withdraw the money tax-free as long as you follow the rules. That's an incredible advantage.

Sure, you put after-tax dollars into your account, but these after-tax dollars grow year after year without being taxed. And when you take them out—if you take them out—there's *still* no tax to pay, so you don't have to worry about where tax rates are heading.

You also have the option to avoid withdrawals altogether, because unlike the traditional IRA, the Roth IRA has no requirement that makes you start withdrawals when you reach 70½.

It's a hard combination to beat, and that's why there's been such a buzz about Roth IRAs. All this might make you wonder how long it can last. Will Congress crack down, as it did with traditional IRAs in 1986? That, however, should be no concern of yours right now.

You can only act according to the rules that are now in place. Worrying about what Congress may do in the future—whether the government may slam the door shut on some of the key Roth benefits—is a waste of time because you can't change the future; you can only act in the present. And with the Roth IRA, there's no better time to convert—and begin taking full advantage of the benefits—like now, as long as you can afford it and you have some time on your side.

For More Information . . .

There are lots of ways you can figure out whether a conversion is best for you. Here are a few:

- T. Rowe Price Associates, a mutual fund group in Baltimore, has a computer software program available for $9.95, including shipping and handling, which can help you decide whether to convert. (To run the program you'll need Windows 3.1 or higher and an IBM compatible PC with at least a 486 processor. The software is available in CD or diskette format.) To order the IRA Analyzer, call 1-800-332-6407. For more about Roth IRAs and conversions, contact the company's Web site at www.troweprice.com.
- The Strong group of mutual funds also has lots of material available on Roth IRAs and Roth IRA conversions plus an online calculator. For information, write: Strong Funds, P.O. Box 2936, Milwaukee, WI 53201, or call 1-800-368-3863, or contact the company's Web site at www.strong funds.com.

Which IRA Is Right for You?

- *Where IRAs fit in your own financial plan*
- *A capsule review of each type of IRA, and a look at some alternatives*
- *The complications of opening and owning an IRA*
- *Penalties and tax rules*
- *Why the benefits of IRAs outweigh the drawbacks*
- *IRAs for children*

Where do IRAs fit in your financial picture?

Once you've set your goals and figured on a way to pay for them, IRAs may help you get where you want to be.

Here's a quick summary look at what each type of IRA is and how IRAs may help—or hinder—you.

The Traditional IRA

If you're saving for retirement, the traditional deductible IRA, which is also known as the regular IRA, or classic IRA, has a lot of appeal.

You'll probably be able to claim a federal income tax deduction for the amount you contribute each year (depending on your overall income level), and the money in your account will grow tax-deferred.

You must have earned income—money from a job—to be able to contribute to a regular IRA. The annual contribution limit is either $2,000 or all of your earned income, whichever is less.

Before you contribute to a regular IRA, first consider options that may be better. For instance, the amount you may contribute to a traditional deductible IRA is generally limited to $2,000 a year. But if you have a 401(k) or 403(b) plan at work, you may be able to contribute far more—as much as $10,000 or more—each year to your account.

You generally get a federal income tax deduction for the amount you contribute, and the money in your account also grows tax-deferred. What's more, 401(k) and 403(b) plans (and similar plans) typically let you invest conveniently through weekly or monthly payroll deductions, for example. Some plans have fairly liberal loan provisions. And when it comes time to withdraw money from these plans, you may be eligible for favorable income tax treatment.

Of course, 401(k) and 403(b) plans typically don't offer anywhere near the type of investment flexibility you get with an IRA. Nor do these plans usually give you the kind of immediate access to your funds that you'd get from an IRA. (You also have more options now to withdraw your IRA money penalty-free.)

Still, because of their convenience and their higher contribution limits, 401(k) plans and 403(b) plans should be your first choice for retirement savings; the traditional IRA, however, may still be used as a supplement.

The Education IRA

If you want to save for your child's education, you may want to set up an education IRA and fully fund it. Remember: You won't get an immediate income tax deduction for the amount you contribute.

However, all the money that your account earns will grow without being taxed each year. And any withdrawals will be free of federal income tax and penalties if you meet the rules. An education IRA alone, however, probably won't be enough to cover all your child's college expenses.

You don't have to have earned income to contribute to an education IRA. (Other types of IRAs require that you have earned income before you can contribute.) Although the education IRA has attractive tax features, the amount you can contribute is limited to just $500 a year, so you may want to use it only as a supplement and consider other investment vehicles to help meet the lion's share of your goal.

Even taxable investments may be a good choice because they may be more flexible and typically don't put a dollar limit on the amount you may contribute. Don't forget, too, that if you withdraw money from an education IRA in a given year to pay for a student's college expenses, you won't also be able to claim the potentially far more valuable Hope Scholarship federal income tax credit or the Lifetime Learning federal income tax credit.

The Roth IRA

The Roth IRA offers an interesting investment alternative that's hard to categorize, making it hard to compare with other options.

If you're saving toward retirement, the deductible IRA is generally a better choice because it gives you the chance to claim an immediate federal income tax deduction; Roth IRAs don't. Over the very long term, however, it's hard to beat the Roth IRA. Although you don't get a deduction, the money in your account grows tax-free, not tax-deferred as with a traditional IRA.

Remember that the most you can contribute to a Roth in any given year is either $2,000 or 100 percent of your earned income, whichever is less.

If you meet the rules, your withdrawals from a Roth account will be totally tax-free and penalty-free. This combination of tax-free earnings and tax-free withdrawals generally gives the Roth IRA a big advantage over the traditional IRA if you're saving for a very long-term goal, such as retirement.

Whether the Roth IRA actually beats the traditional IRA for retirement savings depends on lots of factors, such as how long you have until retirement (for Roth IRAs, the longer the better; traditional IRAs usually win over shorter time frames); whether you invest or spend the tax dollars you save each year with the traditional deductible IRA; and what income tax bracket you'll be in at retirement. The traditional IRA generally wins if you'll be in a lower tax bracket at retirement; the Roth IRA usually wins if you'll be in a higher bracket. If you're in the same bracket when you withdraw as you are when you contribute, either the Roth or the regular IRA may be best depending on which method of calculation you use in your comparison.

To determine which IRA is best, you'll need a worksheet, a calculator, and a lot of patience; there are too many variables to say with certainty which would be best for you. Deciding whether to convert a regular IRA to a Roth IRA also includes a lot of variables and requires a lot of number crunching.

If you have the chance to save at work through a 401(k) or 403(b) plan, do it before you consider contributing to a Roth account. Why? For the same reasons mentioned earlier: because your employer may contribute to your account too and because you generally have the convenience of "forced" saving through payroll deductions. Once you've fully funded your 401(k) or 403(b) plan, then start to think about whether to invest in an IRA—whether a regular IRA or a Roth IRA.

The Nondeductible IRA

If you're thinking about a traditional nondeductible IRA, odds are it's because your income is too high and thus you don't qualify for a fully deductible IRA. If that's the case, your choice is between the nondeductible IRA and the Roth IRA; and the Roth IRA wins hands down.

About the only time you should even think about contributing to a nonde-ductible IRA these days is if your income is so high that you can't get a deduc-tion from a regular IRA and you're not eligible to contribute to a Roth IRA.

Nevertheless, the nondeductible IRA is still worth considering because it gives you the chance to have your money grow tax-deferred. It isn't the only option, though. Some employer-sponsored plans let you contribute after-tax dollars as well as pretax dollars. In effect, these plans give you the chief ben-efit of a nondeductible IRA but often with the convenience of payroll deduc-tions. Nondeductible IRAs are also restricted; you may contribute only up to $2,000 a year (or 100 percent of your earned income, whichever is less).

Are IRAs Always a Good Idea?

By now you probably know just about all you'll ever need to know about IRAs. You've looked at regular IRAs, education IRAs, and Roth IRAs. You've also seen how the nondeductible IRA fits in.

One point to keep in mind: IRAs aren't for everybody.

Sure there's a bag of benefits that comes with almost every type of IRA. You probably know them all by heart. And there are all sorts of tax deductions and tax deferrals and tax-free compounded thingamajigs to take advantage of too. This book has been full of examples of how IRAs can boost your sav-ings to help you pay for a college education, a first house, or just a decent standard of living in retirement.

Great, but forget about the savings benefits and the tax breaks and all the hoopla that you read, hear, and see about IRAs and focus for the moment only on this: Are IRAs right for you? The answer is not necessarily.

Disadvantages of IRAs

As with any investment, IRAs have some disadvantages as well as advan-tages. You're not likely to see them emphasized in advertisements, and sales-people aren't likely to point them out either. But they're there just the same. Here's how some of them shape up:

A Big Step

No matter which type of IRA you finally choose, just opening one is a big step. After all, it's not like stuffing dollar bills into a cookie jar on the kitchen counter. With IRAs, things can get pretty complicated pretty fast.

For starters, there are all sorts of IRAs to consider: Do you want a traditional *deductible* IRA? A traditional *nondeductible* IRA? How about a Roth IRA? Or an education IRA? Then you have to think about where to open one: At the local bank? Credit union? How about a stock brokerage or a mutual fund company?

There may be a lot of paperwork to keep track of and special tax forms to file. And all that's before you think about tax matters.

It's true that IRAs don't require too much work. After all, they really aren't all that exotic. Still, you've got to be willing to commit some time and effort toward your IRAs. Depending on your personal circumstances, time and effort may be just the things you can't come up with right now.

Not Flexible Enough

Want to open a bank account? Just fill out the forms, hand over some cash, and you've pretty much finished the job. It doesn't matter if you had earned income, or taxable compensation, during the year. It doesn't matter how old you are. It doesn't matter what your overall income level is. Just open an account and start earning interest.

Want to take money out of your savings account? No problem. Just write a check. Or stop by the teller window. Or use an ATM card. Easy. It doesn't matter how long the money's been in the account. No formulas are needed to figure out what part of the withdrawal is or isn't taxable. Nobody's bugging you about how old you are or how old your beneficiary is. You just pull out the money and that's that.

Get the point? IRAs may be more flexible than some other types of retirement savings programs, such as 401(k) and 403(b) plans at work, but compared with *all* the other choices in the great big universe of investment choices, IRAs may not be as flexible. In fact, they may seem downright restrictive.

Too Complicated

In 1996, and again in 1997, Congress took some bold steps that dramatically expanded IRAs. As a result, investors were given a lot more choices, rules were relaxed somewhat, and IRAs overall became a lot more appealing. But the expanded IRAs came with a problem: They may still be too complicated for some taxpayers.

Back in the early 1980s, just about everybody who contributed to a regular IRA was able to claim a federal income tax deduction; it was automatic. More important, it was easy to understand. You didn't have to be an accountant to figure out how it worked and whether you'd be eligible. The message was simple and clear: open an IRA, get a deduction.

In 1986 the government changed the rules again. The income tax deduction was no longer automatic. To see if you could get it, you had to take the two-step test: (1) Do you take part in a pension plan at work? (2) Does your adjusted gross income fall below a certain level?

You know what happened next: IRA popularity plunged. The IRA was simply *too complicated.* True, some people couldn't claim the deduction any longer because they had too much income. But many people who *were* eligible to claim the deduction didn't bother with it.

The Rules Became Too Tricky

Some people didn't bother with IRAs because they couldn't spare the money; they needed every dollar just to cover expenses. But it's also true that lots of taxpayers simply didn't bother with the deduction—or with IRAs altogether—because IRAs had become too complicated.

When the government expanded the traditional deductible IRA in 1997, it didn't get rid of the two-step test; it just increased the income hurdles involved in the second part of the test. This meant more taxpayers would be eligible for the deduction over time, but the formula didn't get any simpler. Did the message get any clearer? Nope. So will some people still avoid IRAs just because they're too complicated? Yep.

Tax Complications

One of the reasons IRAs are so attractive to so many people is because they offer tax benefits. That's also one reason some people don't like them. If you're not careful, taxes could rear up and bite you. And the bite could sting. Just look at the possible penalties shown in Figure 14.1.

Too Many Income Limits

Think of all the other things you must consider. For instance, all sorts of income thresholds must be kept in mind—different thresholds for different types of IRAs. For traditional IRAs, tax complications are triggered by withdrawals. Should you withdraw money in the year in which you reach age 70½? Should you wait until the next year and take two withdrawals in one year?

What if you have a Roth IRA and run afoul of the five-year rule by withdrawing money too early?

What if you have an education IRA and you still have money in the account even after you graduate?

Figure 14.1   IRA Penalties

These penalties may apply to your IRA:

- 10 percent penalty on early withdrawals
- 6 percent penalty on excess contributions
- 50 percent penalty for failure to make the required withdrawal
- $50 fine if you make a nondeductible contribution and don't file Form 8606
- $100 for overstating a nondeductible contribution on Form 8606
- 15 percent penalty for prohibited transactions, including:
  - Borrowing money from an IRA
  - Selling property to an IRA
  - Using an IRA as collateral for a loan
  - Buying property for personal use with IRA funds
  - Receiving unreasonable compensation for managing an IRA

Note: "Prohibited transaction" means improper use of your IRA by you, a fiduciary, or member of your family, and could result in more tax and penalties than listed here.
Source: Internal Revenue Service

What are the tax consequences of contributing to a traditional IRA instead of to a Roth IRA? To a Roth IRA instead of to an education IRA? To a nondeductible IRA instead of to a deductible IRA? The tax twists boggle the mind. Remember: It was the Taxpayer Relief Act of 1997, not the Tax Simplification Act.

Too Many Limits Overall

For lots of families, it's a stretch just to come up with the money to contribute to an IRA; the money might be better spent in buying shoes for the children, for example.

For other people, the $2,000 annual contribution limit for traditional IRAs and Roth IRAs and the $500 annual contribution limit on educational IRAs is just too low. For taxpayers who have the financial resources, IRAs simply may not be worth the bother. Why worry about all the penalties, thresholds, and other restrictions and requirements for a relatively small investment?

There's another factor to consider: If you have a traditional IRA, your withdrawals will be taxed as ordinary income, and the highest federal rate on ordinary income is almost 40 percent. So why not just plop a large sum each year (larger than the $2,000 annual IRA limit) into a mutual fund whose performance is linked to an index, such as the Standard & Poor's index of 500 large-company stocks?

Sure, there are tax consequences to that too, but your withdrawals will be treated as capital gains, not as ordinary income, which means they'll generally be subject to lower rates. And the federal capital gains rates aren't as severe as they once were because the government has cut the federal capital gains tax.

Tax Breaks Compared

True, IRAs may offer all sorts of lovely tax benefits. Compared with some other retirement savings plans, however, the breaks aren't quite as appealing.

As mentioned earlier, if you're eligible for a 401(k) or similar plan at work, your employer may be willing to contribute money to your account on your behalf. As a general rule, you'll pay no tax on your employer's contributions, on your contributions, or on your account's earnings until you begin to withdraw money. Even then, you may be eligible for favorable tax treatment.

That's not all. As you know, you generally must start to withdraw money from a traditional IRA by the time you reach age 70½ even if you're still working. But with a 401(k) or other such pension plan, you generally may sidestep this rule as long as you keep working, which means the money in your pension account can continue to grow without being nicked by taxes each year.

Benefits of IRAs

Are IRAs really all that bad? No. But it certainly may seem so if you're left to ponder only the potential disadvantages listed here. For balance, let's do a quick summary of some of the benefits of IRAs.

The IRA is a great way to shelter some of your income from taxation. Got a job? Stick some of your earnings in a traditional IRA. You may be eligible for a federal income tax deduction, and the earnings in your account will grow each year without an immediate tax bite.

Or open a Roth IRA or an education IRA. These two types of IRAs won't provide a tax deduction, but your money will grow tax-free and your withdrawals will come out tax-free as long as you meet the rules. And if you don't qualify for any of these IRAs, there's always the nondeductible IRA, in which your after-tax contributions may grow on a tax-deferred basis.

Penalties Force You to Save

The IRA is a great way to force you to save. Think of the penalties as a lock, or a kind of force field, that'll keep your hands off your money until the time is right.

The IRA is a great way to save toward a long-term goal, such as a college education, the purchase of a house, or a more secure retirement. Got a retirement plan at work already? Use a deductible IRA, a nondeductible IRA, or a Roth IRA as a supplement, a convenient place to stash any extra cash.

If you have a spouse at home, you may set up and contribute to a spousal IRA, which serves as a kind of pension plan for homemakers.

More Flexible than Employer Plans

IRAs are typically more flexible than a lot of retirement savings plans that employers offer. For example, you don't have to make regular contributions to IRAs as you might with a 401(k) plan or 403(b) plan at work. You may make a full annual contribution, a partial contribution, or no contribution to an IRA depending on your circumstances. You don't have to make a contribution annually either; you may contribute money in stages—weekly, monthly, quarterly, or semiannually (depending on what your IRA trustee or custodian allows).

Your Money Is Still Available

IRAs also give you ready access to your money, even though withdrawals may be subject to income tax and penalty. It's good to know nonetheless that you can get your money if you need to. And there are now more ways to tap your IRA penalty-free. Retirement plans at work typically don't offer this kind of flexibility.

You aren't limited to just one IRA with just one IRA trustee or custodian. You may open as many IRAs with as many different financial institutions as your financial resources (and your patience) allow.

Fed up with your bank, brokerage, mutual fund, or insurance company? You may transfer or roll over your IRA from one IRA trustee or custodian to another with relative ease. You're not locked in as you might be with a pension or profit-sharing plan at work; IRAs are typically a lot more portable.

Figure 14.2   Saving for the *Really* Long Haul

Money that's invested in an IRA for your child or grandchild can really add up because many years may pass before the child or grandchild needs the money. All the while, the account grows without being taxed each year. Look how an annual $2,000 investment can grow over time.

	After 20 Years	After 30 Years	After 40 Years
At 5%	$ 69,439	$139,522	$ 253,680
At 8%	98,846	244,692	559,562
At 10%	126,005	361,887	973,704
At 12%	161,398	540,585	1,718,285

Note: The figures assume an investment is made at the start of each year. The child or grandchild must have earned income to contribute to either a regular or Roth IRA. If a regular IRA is used, the child is allowed a deduction, but withdrawals are subject to tax; if a Roth IRA is used, the child gets no deduction, but qualifying withdrawals are tax-free.

A Safe Harbor for Pensions

Lost your job? Changing jobs? Transfer your pension money from your old job directly to a "conduit" IRA. There the money can continue to grow, sheltered from taxation.

If your new job allows it, you can transfer the money from your conduit IRA into your pension plan at your new job. If your new employer doesn't permit this, or if you simply don't get another job, an IRA can still serve as a tax shelter for all the money you've accumulated over the years in your old pension.

Children and IRAs

IRAs can also be of benefit to children and grandchildren. They can be a great way for your child or grandchild to build a tidy sum to help pay for a college education, a first house, or even retirement. (See Figure 14.2).

Your child or grandchild must have money from some sort of job to be able to contribute to either a regular IRA or a Roth IRA (or both) because the same rules about taxable compensation and earned income that apply to you also apply to minors. But this doesn't have to be a big hurdle.

Lots of children or teenagers work as newspaper carriers or babysitters, for example. Maybe they do yard work, repairs, or other odd jobs for neighbors. If not, perhaps you or a family member have a business—even if it's just a sideline business—that could easily hire your teenage child or grandchild for clerical, sorting, packaging, or mailing duties.

The idea, in general, is to have the teen do some work to earn money, because only *earned* income (taxable compensation) counts in determining whether someone is eligible to put money into an IRA. And remember the general rule: The most someone may contribute to an IRA on his or her own behalf is $2,000 *or* 100 percent of his or her earned income, whichever is less. So if a teen earns only $1,000 in a given year, that's the most he or she can invest in an IRA. (It doesn't matter whether the child actually winds up paying taxes on his or her earnings. In fact, odds are the child won't, but he or she still needs earned income in order to contribute to either a Roth or a regular IRA.)

Give a gift to your child or grandchild.   What if your child or grandchild doesn't want to put his or her money into an IRA? Well, first, don't worry because that's a healthy sign. After all, what youngster would really want to lock up all of his or her earnings in an IRA? Odds are that children have plenty of ideas where their money should go, and stashing the cash in a retirement account probably isn't high on the list.

There is a way around this. Why don't you give your child or grandchild enough money to fully fund each year's IRA contribution on condition that the money is actually invested in an IRA? (Parental supervision may be needed.)

Keep in mind that not all IRA custodians or trustees accept IRAs for minors. Some may refuse for legal and other reasons. Others may require a parent to sign off on any contract. Others may require that the child be at least a certain age (such as 14) along with parental approval.

If you're interested, try your local bank, thrift, or credit union. Some of the major stock brokerages allow IRAs for children, and some mutual fund companies do too.

Keep in mind, too, that some institutions will lower their minimum initial investment requirement if the IRA is for a child. (Many mutual fund companies have a lower minimum initial investment for IRAs than for taxable accounts anyway.)

It may also be best to have the child or grandchild open a Roth IRA instead of a regular IRA. Odds are that the federal income tax deduction that comes with a regular IRA won't do much good for a child or teenager. But with the Roth IRA, the child or grandchild will be able to make tax-free withdrawals later on.

Figure 14.3   IRAs at-a-Glance

Here's how individual retirement accounts stack up:

	Regular IRA	Education IRA	Roth IRA
Maximum annual contribution	Yes	Yes	Yes
Earned income required to contribute	Yes	No	Yes
Income tax deduction for contributing	Yes	No	No
Contributions limited by age	Yes	Yes	No
Account earnings grow tax-deferred	Yes	Yes	Yes
Account earnings taxed when withdrawn	Yes	No	No
Early withdrawal penalty	Yes	Yes	Yes
Exceptions to penalty	Yes	Yes	Yes
Withdrawals required	Yes	Yes	No
Penalty if you don't withdraw by deadline	Yes	Yes	No
Rollover/transfer allowed from pensions	Yes	No	No
Rollovers/transfers from other IRAs	Yes	Yes	Yes
Rollovers/transfers to other IRAs	Yes	Yes	Yes

Note: For regular and Roth IRAs, the maximum annual contribution is either $2,000 or 100 percent of your earned income, whichever is less. No earned income is required for an education IRA contribution, and the maximum annual contribution is $500 per beneficiary. You can claim a federal income tax deduction for contributions to a regular IRA if you aren't covered by a pension plan at work; otherwise, the amount of the deduction is based on your modified adjusted gross income. No contribution to a regular IRA can be made after you're 70½; none can be made to an education IRA after the beneficiary is 18.

For a regular IRA, after-tax contributions and account earnings are taxed as ordinary income and may be penalized if withdrawn early; for an education IRA, no tax or penalty on earnings is assessed if it's used for qualifying higher-education expenses before the beneficiary is 30; for a Roth IRA, there is no tax or penalty on earnings if the account is open five years and withdrawals are made after you turn 59½, because of death or disability, or used for first-time homebuyer expenses.

For a regular IRA, minimum required withdrawals must start by April 1 of the year following the year in which you turn 70½; for an education IRA, the account balance must be withdrawn by the beneficiary's 30th birthday or transferred to a family member's education IRA. For regular IRAs, transfer/rollover is okay from or to other regular IRAs; for an education IRA, transfer/rollover is okay from or to other education IRAs; for a Roth IRA, transfer/rollover is okay from or to other Roth IRAs.

To Sum Up . . .

Now you know the rules about IRAs. You know the good points. You know the bad points. You've seen how they may help you or others and how they may hinder you. As a result, you can make a sound decision, one that's firmly grounded in facts and not swayed by advertising hype or a salesperson's smooth talk.

You can also quickly tell that, despite all their complexities, IRAs still have a lot going for them. They're still worth a close look. And if the government continues the pattern set in recent years, we can expect even fewer restrictions—and perhaps more opportunities—from the newly revitalized IRA in the years ahead.

If you have comments or suggestions about this book, you may reach the author at this e-mail address: ndowning@msn.com.

Appendix A
How IRAs Have Evolved

Here are some key moments in the brief history of IRAs:

1974: The Employee Retirement Income Security Act becomes law, reforming the private pension system and creating individual retirement accounts for people not covered by retirement plans.

1976: The Tax Reform Act broadens the annual IRA contribution limit of $1,500 by letting a worker contribute an additional $250 a year for a nonworking spouse.

1978: The Revenue Act creates simplified employee pensions (SEPs) for small businesses, letting employers set up and finance IRAs for workers.

1981: The Economic Recovery Tax Act makes IRAs widely available, vastly expanding their popularity by allowing IRA contributions even by workers already covered by employer-sponsored retirement plans. The law also increases to $2,000 the annual IRA contribution limit.

1986: The Tax Reform Act sharply limits IRAs—and reduces their popularity—by disallowing deductible contributions by workers who are "active participants" in employer-sponsored pension plans unless a worker's adjusted gross income falls below certain dollar limits. The act also creates nondeductible IRAs.

1996: A package of new laws allows penalty-free withdrawals from IRAs for certain medical expenses and health insurance premiums. It also generally expands, to $2,000, the maximum annual IRA contribution for a nonworking spouse (for a new annual limit per couple of $4,000 instead of $2,250) and suspends the 15 percent tax on so-called excess withdrawals from IRAs and other retirement plans.

1997: The Taxpayer Relief Act creates the Roth IRA and education IRA; increases income thresholds a worker uses to determine if IRA contributions are deductible; allows penalty-free early withdrawals for higher-education expenses and first-time homebuyer costs; and repeals the 15 percent tax on excess withdrawals.

Appendix B
Life Expectancy Tables

Table for Determining Applicable Divisor for MDIB*
(Minimum Distribution Incidental Benefit)

Age	Applicable divisor	Age	Applicator divisor
70	26.2	93	8.8
71	25.3	94	8.3
72	24.4	95	7.8
73	23.5	96	7.3
74	22.7	97	6.9
75	21.8	98	6.5
76	20.9	99	6.1
77	20.1	100	5.7
78	19.2	101	5.3
79	18.4	102	5.0
80	17.6	103	4.7
81	16.8	104	4.4
82	16.0	105	4.1
83	15.3	106	3.8
84	14.5	107	3.6
85	13.8	108	3.3
86	13.1	109	3.1
87	12.4	110	2.8
88	11.8	111	2.6
89	11.1	112	2.4
90	10.5	113	2.2
91	9.9	114	2.0
92	9.4	115 and older	1.8

*Use this table if you have a beneficiary other than your spouse who is ten or more years younger than you.

Table I
(Single Life Expectancy)*

Age	Divisor	Age	Divisor
35	47.3	73	13.9
36	46.4	74	13.2
37	45.4	75	12.5
38	44.4	76	11.9
39	43.5	77	11.2
40	42.5	78	10.6
41	41.5	79	10.0
42	40.6	80	9.5
43	39.6	81	8.9
44	38.7	82	8.4
45	37.7	83	7.9
46	36.8	84	7.4
47	35.9	85	6.9
48	34.9	86	6.5
49	34.0	87	6.1
50	33.1	88	5.7
51	32.2	89	5.3
52	31.3	90	5.0
53	30.4	91	4.7
54	29.5	92	4.4
55	28.6	93	4.1
56	27.7	94	3.9
57	26.8	95	3.7
58	25.9	96	3.4
59	25.0	97	3.2
60	24.2	98	3.0
61	23.3	99	2.8
62	22.5	100	2.7
63	21.6	101	2.5
64	20.8	102	2.3
65	20.0	103	2.1
66	19.2	104	1.9
67	18.4	105	1.8
68	17.6	106	1.6
69	16.8	107	1.4
70	16.0	108	1.3
71	15.3	109	1.1
72	14.6	110	1.0

*Table I does not provide for IRA owners younger than 35 years of age. For additional life expectancy tables, see IRS Publication 939.

Table II
(Joint Life and Last Survivor Expectancy)*

Ages	35	36	37	38	39	40	41	42	43	44
35	54.0	53.5	53.0	52.6	52.2	51.8	51.4	51.1	50.8	50.5
36	53.5	53.0	52.5	52.0	51.6	51.2	50.8	50.4	50.1	49.8
37	53.0	52.5	52.0	51.5	51.0	50.6	50.2	49.8	49.5	49.1
38	52.6	52.0	51.5	51.0	50.5	50.0	49.6	49.2	48.8	48.5
39	52.2	51.6	51.0	50.5	50.0	49.5	49.1	48.6	48.2	47.8
40	51.8	51.2	50.6	50.0	49.5	49.0	48.5	48.1	47.6	47.2
41	51.4	50.8	50.2	49.6	49.1	48.5	48.0	47.5	47.1	46.7
42	51.1	50.4	49.8	49.2	48.6	48.1	47.5	47.0	46.6	46.1
43	50.8	50.1	49.5	48.8	48.2	47.6	47.1	46.6	46.0	45.6
44	50.5	49.8	49.1	48.5	47.8	47.2	46.7	46.1	45.6	45.1
45	50.2	49.5	48.8	48.1	47.5	46.9	46.3	45.7	45.1	44.6
46	50.0	49.2	48.5	47.8	47.2	46.5	45.9	45.3	44.7	44.1
47	49.7	49.0	48.3	47.5	46.8	46.2	45.5	44.9	44.3	43.7
48	49.5	48.8	48.0	47.3	46.6	45.9	45.2	44.5	43.9	43.3
49	49.3	48.5	47.8	47.0	46.3	45.6	44.9	44.2	43.6	42.9
50	49.2	48.4	47.6	46.8	46.0	45.3	44.6	43.9	43.2	42.6
51	49.0	48.2	47.4	46.6	45.8	45.1	44.3	43.6	42.9	42.2
52	48.8	48.0	47.2	46.4	45.6	44.8	44.1	43.3	42.6	41.9
53	48.7	47.9	47.0	46.2	45.4	44.6	43.9	43.1	42.4	41.7
54	48.6	47.7	46.9	46.0	45.2	44.4	43.6	42.9	42.1	41.4
55	48.5	47.6	46.7	45.9	45.1	44.2	43.4	42.7	41.9	41.2
56	48.3	47.5	46.6	45.8	44.9	44.1	43.3	42.5	41.7	40.9
57	48.3	47.4	46.5	45.6	44.8	43.9	43.1	42.3	41.5	40.7
58	48.2	47.3	46.4	45.5	44.7	43.8	43.0	42.1	41.3	40.5
59	48.1	47.2	46.3	45.4	44.5	43.7	42.8	42.0	41.2	40.4
60	48.0	47.1	46.2	45.3	44.4	43.6	42.7	41.9	41.0	40.2
61	47.9	47.0	46.1	45.2	44.3	43.5	42.6	41.7	40.9	40.0
62	47.9	47.0	46.0	45.1	44.2	43.4	42.5	41.6	40.8	39.9
63	47.8	46.9	46.0	45.1	44.2	43.3	42.4	41.5	40.6	39.8
64	47.8	46.8	45.9	45.0	44.1	43.2	42.3	41.4	40.5	39.7
65	47.7	46.8	45.9	44.9	44.0	43.1	42.2	41.3	40.4	39.6
66	47.7	46.7	45.8	44.9	44.0	43.1	42.2	41.3	40.4	39.5
67	47.6	46.7	45.8	44.8	43.9	43.0	42.1	41.2	40.3	39.4
68	47.6	46.7	45.7	44.8	43.9	42.9	42.0	41.1	40.2	39.3
69	47.6	46.6	45.7	44.8	43.8	42.9	42.0	41.1	40.2	39.3
70	47.5	46.6	45.7	44.7	43.8	42.9	41.9	41.0	40.1	39.2
71	47.5	46.6	45.6	44.7	43.8	42.8	41.9	41.0	40.1	39.1
72	47.5	46.6	45.6	44.7	43.7	42.8	41.9	40.9	40.0	39.1

Table II (Continued)
(Joint Life and Last Survivor Expectancy)*

Age	35	36	37	38	39	40	41	42	43	44
73	47.5	46.5	45.6	44.6	43.7	42.8	41.8	40.9	40.0	39.0
74	47.5	46.5	45.6	44.6	43.7	42.7	41.8	40.9	39.9	39.0
75	47.4	46.5	45.5	44.6	43.6	42.7	41.8	40.8	39.9	39.0
76	47.4	46.5	45.5	44.6	43.6	42.7	41.7	40.8	39.9	38.9
77	47.4	46.5	45.5	44.6	43.6	42.7	41.7	40.8	39.8	38.9
78	47.4	46.4	45.5	44.5	43.6	42.6	41.7	40.7	39.8	38.9
79	47.4	46.4	45.5	44.5	43.6	42.6	41.7	40.7	39.8	38.9
80	47.4	46.4	45.5	44.5	43.6	42.6	41.7	40.7	39.8	38.8
81	47.4	46.4	45.5	44.5	43.5	42.6	41.6	40.7	39.8	38.8
82	47.4	46.4	45.4	44.5	43.5	42.6	41.6	40.7	39.7	38.8
83	47.4	46.4	45.4	44.5	43.5	42.6	41.6	40.7	39.7	38.8
84	47.4	46.4	45.4	44.5	43.5	42.6	41.6	40.7	39.7	38.8
85	47.4	46.4	45.4	44.5	43.5	42.6	41.6	40.7	39.7	38.8
86	47.3	46.4	45.4	44.5	43.5	42.5	41.6	40.6	39.7	38.8
87	47.3	46.4	45.4	44.5	43.5	42.5	41.6	40.6	39.7	38.7
88	47.3	46.4	45.4	44.5	43.5	42.5	41.6	40.6	39.7	38.7
89	47.3	46.4	45.4	44.4	43.5	42.5	41.6	40.6	39.7	38.7
90	47.3	46.4	45.4	44.4	43.5	42.5	41.6	40.6	39.7	38.7
91	47.3	46.4	45.4	44.4	43.5	42.5	41.6	40.6	39.7	38.7
92	47.3	46.4	45.4	44.4	43.5	42.5	41.6	40.6	39.7	38.7

*Table II does not provide for IRA owners or survivors younger than 35 years of age. For additional life expectancy tables, see IRS Publication 939. If you have a beneficiary other than your spouse who is ten or more years younger than you, see *Minimum Distribution Incident Benefit Requirement.*

Table II (Continued)
(Joint Life and Last Survivor Expectancy)

Age	45	46	47	48	49	50	51	52	53	54
45	44.1	43.6	43.2	42.7	42.3	42.0	41.6	41.3	41.0	40.7
46	43.6	43.1	42.6	42.2	41.8	41.4	41.0	40.6	40.3	40.0
47	43.2	42.6	42.1	41.7	41.2	40.8	40.4	40.0	39.7	39.3
48	42.7	42.2	41.7	41.2	40.7	40.2	39.8	39.4	39.0	38.7
49	42.3	41.8	41.2	40.7	40.2	39.7	39.3	38.8	38.4	38.1
50	42.0	41.4	40.8	40.2	39.7	39.2	38.7	38.3	37.9	37.5
51	41.6	41.0	40.4	39.8	39.3	38.7	38.2	37.8	37.3	36.9
52	41.3	40.6	40.0	39.4	38.8	38.3	37.8	37.3	36.8	36.4
53	41.0	40.3	39.7	39.0	38.4	37.9	37.3	36.8	36.3	35.8
54	40.7	40.0	39.3	38.7	38.1	37.5	36.9	36.4	35.8	35.3
55	40.4	39.7	39.0	38.4	37.7	37.1	36.5	35.9	35.4	34.9
56	40.2	39.5	38.7	38.1	37.4	36.8	36.1	35.6	35.0	34.4
57	40.0	39.2	38.5	37.8	37.1	36.4	35.8	35.2	34.6	34.0
58	39.7	39.0	38.2	37.5	36.8	36.1	35.5	34.8	34.2	33.6
59	39.6	38.8	38.0	37.3	36.6	35.9	35.2	34.5	33.9	33.3
60	39.4	38.6	37.8	37.1	36.3	35.6	34.9	34.2	33.6	32.9
61	39.2	38.4	37.6	36.9	36.1	35.4	34.6	33.9	33.3	32.6
62	39.1	38.3	37.5	36.7	35.9	35.1	34.4	33.7	33.0	32.3
63	38.9	38.1	37.3	36.5	35.7	34.9	34.2	33.5	32.7	32.0
64	38.8	38.0	37.2	36.3	35.5	34.8	34.0	33.2	32.5	31.8
65	38.7	37.9	37.0	36.2	35.4	34.6	33.8	33.0	32.3	31.6
66	38.6	37.8	36.9	36.1	35.2	34.4	33.6	32.9	32.1	31.4
67	38.5	37.7	36.8	36.0	35.1	34.3	33.5	32.7	31.9	31.2
68	38.4	37.6	36.7	35.8	35.0	34.2	33.4	32.5	31.8	31.0
69	38.4	37.5	38.6	35.7	34.9	34.1	33.2	32.4	31.6	30.8
70	38.3	37.4	36.5	35.7	34.8	34.0	33.1	32.3	31.5	30.7
71	38.2	37.3	36.5	35.6	34.7	33.9	33.0	32.2	31.4	30.5
72	38.2	37.3	36.4	35.5	34.6	33.8	32.9	32.1	31.2	30.4
73	38.1	37.2	36.3	35.4	34.6	33.7	32.8	32.0	31.1	30.3
74	38.1	37.2	36.3	35.4	34.5	33.6	32.8	31.9	31.1	30.2
75	38.1	37.1	36.2	35.3	34.5	33.6	32.7	31.8	31.0	30.1
76	38.0	37.1	36,2	35.3	34.4	33.5	32.6	31.8	30.9	30.1
77	38.0	37.1	36.2	35.3	34.4	33.5	32.6	31.7	30.8	30.0
78	38.0	37.0	36.1	35.2	34.3	33.4	32.5	31.7	30.8	29.9
79	37.9	37.0	36.1	35.2	34.3	33.4	32.5	31.6	30.7	29.9
80	37.9	37.0	36.1	35.2	34.2	33.4	32.5	31.6	30.7	29.8
81	37.9	37.0	36.0	35.1	34.2	33.3	32.4	31.5	30.7	29.8
82	37.9	36.9	36.0	35.1	34.2	33.3	32.4	31.5	30.6	29.7

Table II (Continued)
(Joint Life and Last Survivor Expectancy)

Age	45	46	47	48	49	50	51	52	53	54
83	37.9	36.9	36.0	35.1	34.2	33.3	32.4	31.5	30.6	29.7
84	37.8	36.9	36.0	35.1	34.2	33.2	32.3	31.4	30.6	29.7
85	37.8	36.9	36.0	35.1	34.1	33.2	32.3	31.4	30.5	29.6
86	37.8	36.9	36.0	35.0	34.1	33.2	32.3	31.4	30.5	29.6
87	37.8	36.9	35.9	35.0	34.1	33.2	32.3	31.4	30.5	29.6
88	37.8	36.9	35.9	35.0	34.1	33.2	32.3	31.4	30.5	29.6
89	37.8	36.9	35.9	35.0	34.1	33.2	32.3	31.4	30.5	29.6
90	37.8	36.9	35.9	35.0	34.1	33.2	32.3	31.3	30.5	29.6
91	37.8	36.8	35.9	35.0	34.1	33.2	32.2	31.3	30.4	29.5
92	37.8	36.8	35.9	35.0	34.1	33.2	32.2	31.3	30.4	29.5

Appendix B

Table II (continued)
(Joint Life and Last Survivor Expectancy)

Ages	55	56	57	58	59	60	61	62	63	64
55	34.4	33.9	33.5	33.1	32.7	32.3	32.0	31.7	31.4	31.1
56	33.9	33.4	33.0	32.5	32.1	31.7	31.4	31.0	30.7	30.4
57	33.5	33.0	32.5	32.0	31.6	31.2	30.8	30.4	30.1	29.8
58	33.1	32.5	32.0	31.5	31.1	30.6	30.2	29.9	29.5	29.2
59	32.7	32.1	31.6	31.1	30.6	30.1	29.7	29.3	28.9	28.6
60	32.3	31.7	31.2	30.6	30.1	29.7	29.2	28.8	28.4	28.0
61	32.0	31.4	30.8	30.2	29.7	29.2	28.7	28.3	27.8	27.4
62	31.7	31.0	30.4	29.9	29.3	28.8	28.3	27.8	27.3	26.9
63	31.4	30.7	30.1	29.5	28.9	28.4	27.8	27.3	26.9	26.4
64	31.1	30.4	29.8	29.2	28.6	28.0	27.4	26.9	26.4	25.9
65	30.9	30.2	29.5	28.9	28.2	27.6	27.1	26.5	26.0	25.5
66	30.6	29.9	29.2	28.6	27.9	27.3	26.7	26.1	25.6	25.1
67	30.4	29.7	29.0	28.3	27.6	27.0	26.4	25.8	25.2	24.7
68	30.2	29.5	28.8	28.1	27.4	26.7	26.1	25.5	24.9	24.3
69	30.1	29.3	28.6	27.8	27.1	26.5	25.8	25.2	24.6	24.0
70	29.9	29.1	28.4	27.6	26.9	26.2	25.6	24.9	24.3	23.7
71	29.7	29.0	28.2	27.5	26.7	26.0	25.3	24.7	24.0	23.4
72	29.6	28.8	28.1	27.3	26.5	25.8	25.1	24.4	23.8	23.1
73	29.5	28.7	27.9	27.1	26.4	25.6	24.9	24.2	23.5	22.9
74	29.4	28.6	27.8	27.0	26.2	25.5	24.7	24.0	23.3	22.7
75	29.3	28.5	27.7	26.9	26.1	25.3	24.6	23.8	23.1	22.4
76	29.2	28.4	27.6	26.8	26.0	25.2	24.4	23.7	23.0	22.3
77	29.1	28.3	27.5	26.7	25.9	25.1	24.3	23.6	22.8	22.1
78	29.1	28.2	27.4	26.6	25.8	25.0	242	23.4	22.7	21.9
79	29.0	28.2	27.3	26.5	25.7	24.9	24.1	23.3	22.6	21.8
80	29.0	28.1	27.3	26.4	25.6	24.8	24.0	23.2	22.4	21.7
81	28.9	28.1	27.2	26.4	25.5	24.7	23.9	23.1	22.3	21.6
82	28.9	28.0	27.2	26.3	25.5	24.6	23.8	23.0	22.3	21.5
83	28.8	28.0	27.1	26.3	25.4	24.6	23.8	23.0	22.2	21.4
84	28.8	27.9	27.1	26.2	25.4	24.5	23.7	22.9	22.1	21.3
85	28.8	27.9	27.0	26.2	25.3	24.5	23.7	22.8	22.0	21.3
86	28.7	27.9	27.0	26.1	25.3	24.5	23.6	22.8	22.0	21.2
87	28.7	27.8	27.0	26.1	25.3	24.4	23.6	22.8	21.9	21.1
88	28.7	27.8	27.0	26.1	25.2	24.4	23.5	22.7	21.9	21.1
89	28.7	27.8	26.9	26.1	25.2	24.4	23.5	22.7	21.9	21.1
90	28.7	27.8	26.9	26.1	25.2	24.3	23.5	22.7	21.8	21.0
91	28.7	27.8	26.9	26.0	25.2	24.3	23.5	22.6	21.8	21.0
92	28.6	27.8	26.9	26.0	25.2	24.3	23.5	22.6	21.8	21.0

65	66	67	68	69	70	71	72	73	74
25.0	24.6	24.2	23.8	23.4	23.1	22.8	22.5	22.2	22.0
24.6	24.1	23.7	23.3	22.9	22.5	22.2	21.9	21.6	21.4
24.2	23.7	23.2	22.8	22.4	22.0	21.7	21.3	21.0	20.8
23.8	23.3	22.8	22.3	21.9	21.5	21.2	20.8	20.5	20.2
23.4	22.9	22.4	21.9	21.5	21.1	20.7	20.3	20.0	19.6
23.1	22.5	22.0	21.5	21.1	20.6	20.2	19.8	19.4	19.1
22.8	22.2	21.7	21.2	20.7	20.2	19.8	19.4	19.0	18.6
22.5	21.9	21.3	20.8	20.3	19.8	19.4	18.9	18.5	18.2
22.2	21.8	21.0	20.5	20.0	19.4	19.0	18.5	18.1	17.7
22.0	21.4	20.8	20.2	19.6	19.1	18.6	18.2	17.7	17.3
21.8	21.1	20.5	19.9	19.3	18.8	18.3	17.8	17.3	16.9
21.6	20.9	20.3	19.7	19.1	18.5	18.0	17.5	17.0	16.5
21.4	20.7	20.1	19.4	18.8	18.3	17.7	17.2	16.7	16.2
21.2	20.5	19.9	19.2	18.6	18.0	17.5	16.9	16.4	15.9
21.1	20.4	19.7	19.0	18.4	17.8	17.2	16.7	16.1	15.6
21.0	20.2	19.5	18.9	18.2	17.6	17.0	16.4	15.9	15.4
20.8	20.1	19.4	18.7	18.1	17.4	16.8	16.2	15.7	15.1
20.7	20.0	19.3	18.6	17.9	17.3	16.6	16.0	15.5	14.9
20.6	19.9	19.2	18.5	17.8	17.1	16.5	15.9	15.3	14.7
20.5	19.8	19.1	18.4	17.7	17.0	16.3	15.7	15.1	14.5
20.5	19.7	19.0	18.3	17.6	16.9	16.2	15.6	15.0	14.4
20.4	19.6	18.9	18.2	17.5	16.8	16.1	15.5	14.8	14.2
20.4	19.6	18.8	18.1	17.4	16.7	16.0	15.4	14.7	14.1
20.3	19.5	18.8	18.0	17.3	16.6	15.9	15.3	14.6	14.0
20.3	19.5	18.7	18.0	17.2	16.5	15.8	15.2	14.5	13.9
20.2	19.4	18.7	17.9	17.2	16.5	15.8	15.1	14.5	13.8
20.2	19.4	18.6	17.9	17.1	16.4	15.7	15.0	14.4	13.7
20.2	19.4	18.6	17.8	17.1	16.4	15.7	15.0	14.3	13.7

Table II (continued)
(Joint Life and Last Survivor Expectancy)

Ages	55	56	57	58	59	60	61	62	63	64
93	28.6	27.8	26.9	26.0	25.1	24.3	23.4	22.6	21.8	20.9
94	28.6	27.7	26.9	26.0	25.1	24.3	23.4	22.6	21.7	20.9
95	28.6	27.7	26.9	26.0	25.1	24.3	23.4	22.6	21.7	20.9
96	28.6	27.7	26.9	26.0	25.1	24.2	23.4	22.6	21.7	20.9
97	28.6	27.7	26.8	26.0	25.1	24.2	23.4	22.5	21.7	20.9
98	28.6	27.7	26.8	26.0	25.1	24.2	23.4	22.5	21.7	20.9
99	28.6	27.7	26.8	26.0	25.1	24.2	23.4	22.5	21.7	20.9
100	28.6	27.7	26.8	26.0	25.1	24.2	23.4	22.5	21.7	20.8
101	28.6	27.7	26.8	25.9	25.1	24.2	23.4	22.5	21.7	20.8
102	28.6	27.7	26.8	25.9	25.1	24.2	23.3	22.5	21.7	20.8
103	28.6	27.7	26.8	25.9	25.1	24.2	23.3	22.5	21.7	20.8
104	28.6	27.7	26.8	25.9	25.1	24.2	23.3	22.5	21.6	20.8
105	28.6	27.7	26.8	25.9	25.1	24.2	23.3	22.5	21.6	20.8
106	28.6	27.7	26.8	25.9	25.1	24.2	23.3	22.5	21.6	20.8
107	28.6	27.7	26.8	25.9	25.1	24.2	23.3	22.5	21.6	20.8
108	28.6	27.7	26.8	25.9	25.1	24.2	23.3	22.5	21.6	20.8
109	28.6	27.7	26.8	25.9	25.1	24.2	23.3	22.5	21.6	20.8
110	28.6	27.7	26.8	25.9	25.1	24.2	23.3	22.5	21.6	20.8
111	28.6	27.7	26.8	25.9	25.0	24.2	23.3	22.5	21.6	20.8
112	28.6	27.7	26.8	25.9	25.0	24.2	23.3	22.5	21.6	20.8
113	28.6	27.7	26.8	25.9	25.0	24.2	23.3	22.5	21.6	20.8
114	28.6	27.7	26.8	25.9	25.0	24.2	23.3	22.5	21.6	20.8
115	28.6	27.7	26.8	25.9	25.0	24.2	23.3	22.5	21.6	20.8

65	66	67	68	69	70	71	72	73	74
20.1	19.3	18.6	17.8	17.1	16.3	15.6	14.9	14.3	13.6
20.1	19.3	18.5	17.8	17.0	16.3	15.6	14.9	14.2	13.6
20.1	19.3	18.5	17.8	17.0	16.3	15.6	14.9	14.2	13.5
20.1	19.3	18.5	17.7	17.0	16.2	15.5	14.8	14.2	13.5
20.1	19.3	18.5	17.7	17.0	16.2	15.5	14.8	14.1	13.5
20.1	19.3	18.5	17.7	16.9	16.2	15.5	14.8	14.1	13.4
20.0	19.2	18.5	17.7	16.9	16.2	15.5	14.7	14.1	13.4
20.0	19.2	18.4	17.7	16.9	16.2	15.4	14.7	14.0	13.4
20.0	19.2	18.4	17.7	16.9	16.1	15.4	14.7	14.0	13.3
20.0	19.2	18.4	17.6	16.9	16.1	15.4	14.7	14.0	13.3
20.0	19.2	18.4	17.6	16.9	16.1	15.4	14.7	14.0	13.3
20.0	19.2	18.4	17.6	16.9	16.1	15.4	14.7	14.0	13.3
20.0	19.2	18.4	17.6	16.9	16.1	15.4	14.6	13.9	13.3
20.0	19.2	18.4	17.6	16.9	16.1	15.3	14.6	13.9	13.3
20.0	19.2	18.4	17.6	16.9	16.1	15.3	14.6	13.9	13.2
20.0	19.2	18.4	17.6	16.9	16.1	15.3	14.6	13.9	13.2
20.0	19.2	18.4	17.6	16.9	16.1	15.3	14.6	13.9	13.2
20.0	19.2	18.4	17.6	16.9	16.1	15.3	14.6	13.9	13.2
20.0	19.2	18.4	17.6	16.9	16.0	15.3	14.6	13.9	13.2
20.0	19.2	18.4	17.6	16.9	16.0	15.3	14.6	13.9	13.2
20.0	19.2	18.4	17.6	16.9	16.0	15.3	14.6	13.9	13.2
20.0	19.2	18.4	17.6	16.9	16.0	15.3	14.6	13.9	13.2
20.0	19.2	18.4	17.6	16.9	16.0	15.3	14.6	13.9	13.2

Table II (continued)
(Joint Life and Last Survivor Expectancy)

Ages	75	76	77	78	79	80	81	82	83	84
75	16.5	16.1	15.8	15.4	15.1	14.9	14.6	14.4	14.2	14.0
76	16.1	15.7	15.4	15.0	14.7	14.4	14.1	13.9	13.7	13.5
77	15.8	15.4	15.0	14.6	14.3	14.0	13.7	13.4	13.2	13.0
78	15.4	15.0	14.6	14.2	13.9	13.5	13.2	13.0	12.7	12.5
79	15.1	14.7	14.3	13.9	13.5	13.2	12.8	12.5	12.3	12.0
80	14.9	14.4	14.0	13.5	13.2	12.8	12.5	12.2	11.9	11.6
81	14.6	14.1	13.7	13.2	12.8	12.5	12.1	11.8	11.5	11.2
82	14.4	13.9	13.4	13.0	12.5	12.2	11.8	11.5	11.1	10.9
83	14.2	13.7	13.2	12.7	12.3	11.9	11.5	11.1	10.8	10.5
84	14.0	13.5	13.0	12.5	12.0	11.6	11.2	10.9	10.5	10.2
85	13.8	13.3	12.8	12.3	11.8	11.4	11.0	10.6	10.2	9.9
86	13.7	13.1	12.6	12.1	11.6	11.2	10.8	10.4	10.0	9.7
87	13.5	13.0	12.4	11.9	11.4	11.0	10.6	10.1	9.8	9.4
88	13.4	12.8	12.3	11.8	11.3	10.8	10.4	10.0	9.6	9.2
89	13.3	12.7	12.2	11.6	11.1	10.7	10.2	9.8	9.4	9.0
90	13.2	12.6	12.1	11.5	11.0	10.5	10.1	9.6	9.2	8.8
91	13.1	12.5	12.0	11.4	10.9	10.4	9.9	9.5	9.1	8.7
92	13.1	12.5	11.9	11.3	10.8	10.3	9.8	9.4	8.9	8.5
93	13.0	12.4	11.8	11.3	10.7	10.2	9.7	9.3	8.8	8.4
94	12.9	12.3	11.7	11.2	10.6	10.1	9.6	9.2	8.7	8.3
95	12.9	12.3	11.7	11.1	10.6	10.1	9.6	9.1	8.6	8.2
96	12.9	12.2	11.6	11.1	10.5	10.0	9.5	9.0	8.5	8.1
97	12.8	12.2	11.6	11.0	10.5	9.9	9.4	8.9	8.5	8.0
98	12.8	12.2	11.5	11.0	10.4	9.9	9.4	8.9	8.4	8.0
99	12.7	12.1	11.5	10.9	10.4	9.8	9.3	8.8	8.3	7.9
100	12.7	12.1	11.5	10.9	10.3	9.8	9.2	8.7	8.3	7.8
101	12.7	12.1	11.4	10.8	10.3	9.7	9.2	8.7	8.2	7.8
102	12.7	12.0	11.4	10.8	10.2	9.7	9.2	8.7	8.2	7.7
103	12.6	12.0	11.4	10.8	10.2	9.7	9.1	8.6	8.1	7.7
104	12.6	12.0	11.4	10.8	10.2	9.6	9.1	8.6	8.1	7.6
105	12.6	12.0	11.3	10.7	10.2	9.6	9.1	8.5	8.0	7.6
106	12.6	11.9	11.3	10.7	10.1	9.6	9.0	8.5	8.0	7.5
107	12.6	11.9	11.3	10.7	10.1	9.6	9.0	8.5	8.0	7.5
108	12.6	11.9	11.3	10.7	10.1	9.5	9.0	8.5	8.0	7.5
109	12.6	11.9	11.3	10.7	10.1	9.5	9.0	8.4	7.9	7.5
110	12.6	11.9	11.3	10.7	10.1	9.5	9.0	8.4	7.9	7.4
111	12.5	11.9	11.3	10.7	10.1	9.5	8.9	8.4	7.9	7.4
112	12.5	11.9	11.3	10.6	10.1	9.5	8.9	8.4	7.9	7.4
113	12.5	11.9	11.2	10.6	10.0	9.5	8.9	8.4	7.9	7.4
114	12.5	11.9	11.2	10.6	10.0	9.5	8.9	8.4	7.9	7.4
115	12.5	11.9	11.2	10.6	10.0	9.5	8.9	8.4	7.9	7.4

85	86	87	88	89	90	91	92	93	94
9.6	9.3	9.1	8.9	8.7	8.5	8.3	8.2	8.0	7.9
9.3	9.1	8.8	8.6	8.3	8.2	8.0	7.8	7.7	7.6
9.1	8.8	8.5	8.3	8.1	7.9	7.7	7.5	7.4	7.2
8.9	8.6	8.3	8.0	7.8	7.6	7.4	7.2	7.1	6.9
8.7	8.3	8.1	7.8	7.5	7.3	7.1	6.9	6.8	6.6
8.5	8.2	7.9	7.6	7.3	7.1	6.9	6.7	6.5	6.4
8.3	8.0	7.7	7.4	7.1	6.9	6.7	6.5	6.3	6.2
8.2	7.8	7.5	7.2	6.9	6.7	6.5	6.3	6.1	5.9
8.0	7.7	7.4	7.1	6.8	6.5	6.3	6.1	5.9	5.8
7.9	7.6	7.2	6.9	6.6	6.4	6.2	5.9	5.8	5.6
7.8	7.5	7.1	6.8	6.5	6.3	6.0	5.8	5.6	5.4
7.7	7.3	7.0	6.7	6.4	6.1	5.9	5.7	5.5	5.3
7.6	7.3	6.9	6.6	6.3	6.0	5.8	5.5	5.3	5.1
7.6	7.2	6.8	6.5	6.2	5.9	5.6	5.4	5.2	5.0
7.5	7.1	6.7	6.4	6.1	5.8	5.5	5.3	5.1	4.9
7.4	7.0	6.6	6.3	6.0	5.7	5.4	5.2	5.0	4.8
7.3	6.9	6.6	6.2	5.9	5.6	5.3	5.1	4.9	4.7
7.3	6.9	6.5	6.2	5.8	5.5	5.3	5.0	4.8	4.6
7.2	6.8	6.4	6.1	5.8	5.5	5.2	4.9	4.7	4.5
7.2	6.8	6.4	6.0	5.7	5.4	5.1	4.8	4.6	4.4
7.1	6.7	6.3	6.0	5.6	5.3	5.0	4.8	4.5	4.3
7.1	6.7	6.3	5.9	5.6	5.3	5.0	4.7	4.5	4.2
7.1	6.6	6.2	5.9	5.5	5.2	4.9	4.6	4.4	4.2
7.0	6.6	6.2	5.8	5.5	5.2	4.9	4.6	4.3	4.1
7.0	6.6	6.2	5.8	5.5	5.1	4.8	4.5	4.3	4.1
7.0	6.6	6.2	5.8	5.4	5.1	4.8	4.5	4.3	4.0
7.0	6.5	6.1	5.7	5.4	5.1	4.8	4.5	4.2	4.0
7.0	6.5	6.1	5.7	5.4	5.0	4.7	4.4	4.2	3.9
6.9	6.5	6.1	5.7	5.4	5.0	4.7	4.4	4.2	3.9
6.9	6.5	6.1	5.7	5.3	5.0	4.7	4.4	4.1	3.9
6.9	6.5	6.1	5.7	5.3	5.0	4.7	4.4	4.1	3.9

Index

A

AAII Journal, 49
Account, opening an IRA, 38–39
Adjusted gross income, and IRA deduction, 30
Administrative fees, 50
Age limit, on IRAs, 27–28
American Association of Individual Investors, 49
Annuities, 123
Assets, 8

B

Balance sheet, 8–10
Basis, elimination of, 89–90
Beneficiary, of IRA, 77, 80
    choosing, 87
    life expectancy tables and, 77–78, 81–83
    naming, 86–87
    no early withdrawal penalty for, 90
    relationship of, to IRA owner, 91–93
    Roth IRAs and, 136, 142, 147
Bunching withdrawals, 72–73

C

Cash flow statement, 10–13
Charitable donations, 88
Children, and IRAs, 163–64
College costs
    see also Education IRA
    early withdrawal from IRA and, 62, 64
Compounding, 23–24, 67, 98
    Roth IRA and, 119
Conduit IRA, 58
Contribution limit, 26–27
Custodial fees, 50

D

Deadline, for contributions, 28–29, 54
Death, and IRA early withdrawals, 62, 63
Debts, 8

Deductible IRAs, 17
Deduction, claiming an IRA, 21–22, 51–52
    adjusted gross income and, 30–31
    formula for determining, 34–35
Die Rich and Tax Free, 95
Direct rollovers, 54, 56–57
Disability, and early withdrawal, 62, 63
Disability insurance, 14
Disclaiming interest, 94
Diversification, 13, 41–42, 47
Dividend reinvestment plans, 45, 46, 49
Divorce or maintenance agreement, early IRA withdrawal and, 65
Dollar limit, on IRAs, 26–27

E

Early contributions, 28–29
Economic Recovery Tax Act, 167
Education IRA, 6, 104–16, 155, 167
    alternatives to, 112–13
    cashing in, 108
    income limits, 107
    limits on type of school, 108
    points to consider, 111–12
    problems with, 105–6
    resources, 116
    tax breaks, 107
    transferring money from, 110
    withdrawing from, 109
Employee Retirement Income Security Act, 167
Employee retirement savings plans, 102, 154–55, 161, 162
    and Roth IRAs, 135, 156
    estimating retirement needs and, 17
    IRA contributions and, 29–30
Ernst & Young, 137

Estate planning, 86–95
    beneficiary of estate, 86–87, 90–93
    elimination of basis with IRAs, 89–90
    importance of, 93–94
    resources, 95
    taxes, 88–89
Estate Planning Made Easy, 95
Everyone's Money Book, 19
Excess withdrawals, 167

F

Federal estate tax, 88
Federal insurance, 39
Fees, avoiding, 50–51
Fidelity Funds, 137
Fidelity Investments, 59
Fidelity Retirement Planning Guide, 59
Financial plan, 7–19
    estimating retirement needs, 16–17
    income statement, 10–13
    IRAs and, 15–16, 17
    long-range goals, 14–15
    personal balance sheet, 8–10
    resources, 18–19
    savings plans, 13–14
Financing College: Planning for Your Child's Education, 116
First-time homebuying costs, 62, 65
    Roth IRAs and, 121, 122
Flexibility, and IRAs, 38, 48, 55, 59

G

Gift tax, 93
Goals, long-range, 14–15
Gold, 46
Goodman, Jordan E., 19
Grandchildren, and IRAs, 163–65

H

Health insurance, early withdrawal from IRA and, 62, 64

History, of IRAs, 167
Homebuying expense (first
time)
early withdrawal from
IRA and, 62, 65
Roth IRAs and, 121, 122
Homemakers, and IRAs, 5
Hope Scholarship Credit, 111,
116, 130, 144

I

Income
limits, 4–5
sources of, 10
statement, 10–13
withdrawals seen as, 67
Income in respect of a
decedent, 94
Inflows, 10
Inherited IRAs, 90, 91–93, 94
Institute of Certified
Financial Planners, 18, 116
*Investing Your Retirement Plan
Distribution,* 59
Investment Company
Institute, 49
Investment portfolio, balance
of, 13
Investment, of IRA dollars,
37–49
in larger financial
picture, 47
mutual fund, choosing,
42–43
opening an account, 38–
40
options, 40–41
professional
management and
diversification, 41–42
resources, 49
stock brokerage,
choosing, 43–44
stock investment direct,
44–46
terms and conditions of
account, 37–38
time horizon, 47–48
variety of choices, 46
IRAs
benefits of, 161–65
disadvantages of, 157–61
management of, 50–59
avoiding fees, 50–51
deadlines, 54
deductions, 51–52
pension to IRA switch,

50–57
rollover IRAs, 52–54
transferring your IRA,
52
options available with,
4–6
qualifying for, 26–36
age limit, 27–28
Congressional rules,
31–33
deadlines, 28–29
dollar limit, 26–27
figuring your
deduction, 34–35
resources, 36
two-part test, 29–31
tax breaks, 20–25
claiming your
deduction, 21–22
postponing your tax
bill, 23–25
types of, 154–57
IRS Booklets
college savings plans, 116
*Individual Retirement
Arrangements* (#590),
36
*Introduction of Estate and
Gift Taxes* (#950), 95
nondeductible IRAs, 103
*Tax Information for
Survivors, Executors,
and Administrators*
(#559), 95

J

Joint Life and Last Survivor
Expectancy table, 75, 78,
170–79

K

Kaye, Barry, 95

L

Life expectancy tables, 72, 74–
78, 81, 168–79
joint life and last
survivor expectancy,
75, 78, 170–79
minimum distribution
incidental benefit,
81–83, 168
single life expectancy,
76–77, 169
Life insurance, 13–14

Lifetime Learning Credit, 111,
116, 130, 144
Lump-sum distribution, 58

M

Maintenance fees, 50
Management, of IRAs, 50–59
avoiding fees, 50–51
conduit IRA, 58
deductions, 51–52
flexibility, of IRAs, 55
pension to IRA switch,
56–57
resources, 59
rolling over your IRA,
52–54
transferring your IRA, 52
Mandatory withdrawals, 61,
68–70
Married couples, IRA tax
breaks and, 21–22, 33
Medical expenses, and early
withdrawal, 62, 64, 167
Merrill Lynch, 137
Minimum distribution
incidental benefit table, 81–
83, 168
Minimum withdrawals, 71–
85
choosing a method for,
79–80
first withdrawal, 72–73
how much to withdraw,
74
life expectancy tables
and, 81
methods for, 79–80
minimum distribution
incidental benefit table
and, 82–83
rules summary, 71
Minus One method, 79
Modified adjusted gross
income, 33
Morningstar, 42
Mutual Fund Education
Alliance, 49
Mutual funds, 41–43, 68
choosing, 42–43
college expenses and, 114

N

Net worth, determining, 10
No-Load Stock Insider
newsletter, 49
No-load stock programs, 46

Nondeductible IRAs, 18, 96–
103, 156–57
advantages of, 98–99
compounding, 98
Congress and, 102
options, 102–3
resources, 103
Roth IRAs, 102. *See also*
Roth IRAs
rules, 99–101
taxes, 96–98
Nonspouse beneficiary, 92
Nonworking spouses, and
IRAs, 5, 34–35

O

Online opening, of IRA, 44
Outflows, 10

P

Pension to IRA switch, 56–57
Phillips, David T., 95
Precious metals, 46
Premature withdrawal
penalty, 60, 61–66
Probate process, 86

Q

Qualified distribution, 121

R

Recalculation method, 79–80
Required beginning date, 72
Required minimum
distribution, 72
Retirement needs, estimating,
16–17
Retirement plans
401(k) and 403(b), 102,
154–55, 156, 161, 162
and Roth IRAs, 135
estimating retirement
needs, 17
IRA contributions and,
29–30
Revenue Act, 167
Rollover IRA, 52–54
Roth IRAs, 5, 17, 102, 117–52,
156, 167
beneficiaries of, 136, 142,
148
benefits of, 117–18
converting to, 139–53
avoiding tax and
penalty, 146–47
decision for, 147–49

high growth search,
150
limits on, 142–45
options when, 145–46
process of, 141–42
resources, 153
tax breaks, 139–40
variables, 151–52
details, 118–19
education expenses and,
112–13
guidelines, 129–35
income limits, 120
resources, 137
rules, 121, 125–26
and stocks compared,
127
and taxable accounts
compared, 126–27
tax benefits, 121–24,
139–40
taxation on earnings,
124–25
and traditional IRAs
compared, 128
Roth, William V., Jr., 119

S

Sandlun, Bruce G., 69
Savings plans, maximizing,
13–14
Self-directed IRA, 43–44
Series of early IRA
withdrawals, 63
Single Life Expectancy table,
76–77, 169
Social Security benefits, 16, 67
Roth IRAs and, 148
*Special Report: The New Tax
Legislation*, 137
Spouse, as IRA beneficiary,
88, 91–92
Statement of cash flow, 10–13
Stock brokerage, 43–44
Stock investments, 40–41
direct, 44–46
Stock mutual funds, and Roth
IRAs, 150
Stocks, and Roth IRAs
compared, 127
Strong Funds, 25, 153
Success tax, 67, 169

T

T. Rowe Price Associates, 137,
153

T. Rowe Price IRA Analyzer,
137, 153
*T. Rowe Price Retirees Financial
Guide*, 19
Tax basis, elimination of,
89–90
Tax Reform Act of 1986, 29,
128, 167
Taxes
nondeductible IRAs and,
96–98
tax breaks, with IRAs,
20–25
withdrawing money
from IRA and, 61–68
Taxpayer Relief Act of 1997,
4, 6, 128, 167
IRA deductions and,
31–33
success tax and, 67
Ten percent penalty on early
withdrawal, 60, 61–66
Timely withdrawals of IRA
money, 66
Traditional IRA, 154–55
Transfer of IRA money, 5, 52,
53, 65
Two-part test, 29–31

U

*Understanding the Taxpayer
Relief Act of 1997*, 6

V

Value Line Mutual Fund
Survey, 42
Vanguard Funds, 6, 116, 137
Ventura, John, 95

W

Will Kit, The, 95
Withdrawing money, 5,
60–70, 160
avoiding penalty on
early withdrawal, 60,
61–66
mandatory withdrawal,
61, 68–70
nondeductible IRAs and,
99–101
Roth IRAs and, 122–26,
145–46
tax consequences, 60,
66–68
Wolfkiel, Bill, 95